Surfing Brilliant Corners

Sam Bleakley
photos JS Callahan

Alison Hodge

The new generation – Cap-Haïtien, Haiti

For Lola and Sandy, Mum and Dad, Grandpa, Brioney, Phaedra, Jonty, Amelie, Isobel, Caitlin and Kara.

'You will never know how wonderful it is to stand on top of the highest mountains until you have been in the deepest valleys.'
My late, great geography teacher, Barry Blamey

Acknowledgements
Thank you Oxbow, Chapel Idne Surf Shop, Vans, Surftech, *The Surfer's Path* and *Carve*.

Contents

1 Setting the Pace

If the pulse of jazz is the ocean swell, then the surfer is the soloist improvising against that backdrop, creating space through style and timing. Blue notes ring out against a grinding ocean bass. There is the sustained work of the drummer: rolls on the tom-toms, a crackling snare drum, hits to the high-hat, and spectacular cymbal splashes as the waves rise, fold and smack rim-shots down the line. The green water with its white hair is combed back by a stiff offshore. It races up the sand and sucks back like brushes caressing the skins. A melody, the theme of regular sets, impregnates the air. It mixes synaesthetically with the smell of stirred seaweed, hints of sulphur, and tastes of raked salt. This is the opening theme, stated and repeated in brilliant corners all over the world. It is a precursor to a long line of improvisation before the deep low pressure's effect passes and perfect swell disappears, fading to quiet. The surfer is the fifth member of the quintet, together with wind, swell, current and moving bodies of seawater.

Another Atlantic set wave rises to its full height, pulling invisible threads and gathering as a dense cloud of spray. An off-white line scars the channel that runs out past the rocks, and I scan the set-up and pattern of rips from the cliff top. A kestrel wheels overhead, then locks into a hover, rippling, and concentrates the long gaze down, perfectly still, in absolute poise. The bird suddenly drops, tips the ground, and wheels away with a catch in its talons. I run down the steep path, where the granite skirts the sea. The gorse throws out its coconut and pineapple pungency with a top note of vanilla – a piña-colada halo.

I reach the water's edge and put on my leash. The shorebreak is veined with vivid greens, pale blues and milky turquoise, against which the bobbing cormorant is a stark black punctuation mark. The bird briefly catches my eye, and then dives, unlocking the sentence. The sea's language is eddies and vortices, that every surfer learns through experience, and I use now to help me paddle out to the deepest take-off point, striking up a conversation with the rising swell and getting into the rhythm already set by the band that has been up all night, rehearsing without me. I duck under the next cracking beauty of a new set, noting again how much the swell is increasing. The water doubles over, and on the other side of the wave I bask in a temporary rainbow as the wind picks off the crest in a fragile, but continuous sheet. After the set passes, a big noiseless space opens up, and there is a familiar calm. Time expands. I am alive and wired, wet-nested at the rim of Gwenver, the north end of Sennen, the westerly tip of Cornwall and Britain, suspended between fish and bird, surfing a brilliant corner with jazz in mind.

Keeping up with the drummer – Western Sahara

Picking out a green-engined, roiling wave, I paddle into position, rising on the sea's stretching skin. Caught between gravity and levity, my first fin catches, and I lock in, compress, let the board bite and accelerate as a sweet sound emerges. Not a hum, or a vibration, but a long note held on circular breathing, tonally just right. Now driving up the face in a honking John Coltrane solo, I cut back in a big arc and, for a split second, am hovering like a blue note that falls, ripe, from the bell of Miles Davis' horn, languishing just behind the beat. I see the curtain falling ahead and cross-step quickly to the front of the board in the manner of the sweet'n'sour harmolodics of Ornette Coleman, and, with five toes rolled over the nose, throw a Black Panther salute soul arch as a blistering Art Blakey drum solo nearly chases me down. The poise of the kestrel lingers in my mind. I kick out elegantly – the compressed coda – over the turbine that hurls itself in a last gasp at the mashed-up mica and quartz in the continual creation of beachfront. I half expect to see a school of dolphins right behind me to cap the session, but there is just openness, a space between tracks, the lingering satisfaction of a gig played well, and I fully savour the moment.

Home turf – Gwenver, West Cornwall

In the Cornish language, there is a word for the ever-present grind of the sea – *mordros*. The late, great jazz drummer Art Blakey might have called it 'the Big Beat', after his thundering style. Set against this background drive is the single feathering wave – *mordon* – that is a feminine word. The wave rises, heavy and thick at the base, light and crisp at the lip as it peaks and throws, breaking free from the anchor that is the deep swell, the incessant tidal motion, the undercurrent, the pulse, the bass-line. As the wave throws bright foamheads, it plays an improvised run against the background *mordros*, round blue notes against a big beat. Waves are a delicate *presence* weaved into the sea's *force*. To meet this graceful presence surfers need poise. Good musicians know all about poise. They call it 'timing'. It is most obvious in jazz, where a soloist improvises around the rhythmic groundswell of bass and drums. In those magic surf sessions where timing seems just right, poised on that small sliver that is the surfboard, against this massive, shifting backdrop that stretches to the horizon, I am, again, both fish and bird, knowing the world through waves and their music.

6 Setting the Pace

For his pioneering album *Brilliant Corners*, the genius pianist Thelonius Monk wrote music that was so difficult it was practically unplayable by his fellow band members, and one track had to be pieced together by sound engineers from several takes. This is the kind of challenge that the wild, unfurling ocean presents to surfers: the music it makes is often impossible to follow, but surfing is about improvising in brilliant ways that utilize the sea's surprises.

Most surf sessions go unrecorded, unnoticed, but remain as vivid memories. The local crew may hoot once in a while or pass a comment, but mostly the band you play with is the temporary, single wave and its trajectory to the final chorus. As you paddle back out, the drummers on that last six-wave set have long since packed their kits and gone home. Each kit is unpacked, whole, in a crash of cymbals and a final crackle of snare drum and ringing rim-shot as the lip drives to sand. Nobody hears your silent solos. So why do it if you do not have an audience? In professional contest surfing, I need the audience to spur me on. But in these soul sessions my witness is bird life, or, on a lucky day, sea-life. I am swooping with the kestrel and dropping like a stone to catch a claw on the wave face and edge up to the lip, hooting and howling like the animals, my board speed-rattling against the slower grind of the sea. And I have rehearsed this art of surfing until it hurts, living and breathing this wild beachbreak at home in Gwenver in particular.

I am infected by this so-called 'sport', that is so much more. The music of the moment and my relationship to this accompanying band is not simply born of improvisation, but is based on resolute practice. It has been my job, as a professional surfer, for over ten years. I have loved the job, but it demands dedication, avoiding pride or arrogance and experiencing shame and humility. And days like this – with predictable six-wave sets, 12 minutes between sets, and third wave in each set the biggest – are rare. Mostly I am surfing cold, blown-out conditions just to keep in shape for trips abroad, or competitions. But today I have the wished-for confluence of the local band on top form, and accompanying solos that hit the mark, gain a beautiful curve, an inflection, a round tone.

As I write this, I am just 30 – but I have a story to tell. It is based around surfing, being passionately involved with the ocean and her moods, and coming to know brilliant corners of the world, to form an ecological awareness. Sports professionals suffer a paradox: their careers usually have a short trajectory, and they may peak in the first quarter of their lives. They have a sports story to tell, but without the wealth of life experience to inform it. I am in that position. My sport, however, has provided me with a ticket to visit places that studying geography academically had only introduced me to on paper. In a short time I have accumulated many stories, some profound, some simply comical. But am I not simply adding to the misery by writing about my travels when my life has really only just begun?

Overleaf: Cymbal splash – Barbado

My rationale is that this story about 'my' life is not really about me. It is about the experiences that have formed me, and these experiences are more common than you might think.

This is a tale of two identities: fish and ocean-roaming bird, surfer and traveller. These interweave and feed each other. This book is my soul arch, attempting to bridge fish and bird through metaphors of jazz. My first love was the ocean, so as a kid I often wished I were a fish, bathed in that plasma, tangled in seaweed, wrapped in that often bitterly cold, thin, green oil. I would watch my dad surfing: he had a minimalist style, instantly recognizable – an all-or-nothing quick paddle, arms like windmills that transformed to a floating glide. Mum, my sisters and I collected bleached cuttlefish bones and purple shells, where the strandline was beaded with violet jellyfish drying out in the midday sun.

At high tide, the waves stopped breaking, and Dad paddled in from the surf. We would swim together in the shorebreak that always seemed to be infested with sea lice. They gnawed at me, and the shore-dump unloaded and drew back dramatically, taking sheets of sand with it. I loved to get sucked back and then hurled up the beach by the next wave. I remember how the sound of the sea rang around, bouncing back from the cliff faces. I felt that I needed this drumming on sand, the ozone clouds it raised, and the rhythm of the tides, to be truly alive. I wanted to be cloaked in the saline, hugged tight by the water. Oddly, this felt like safety, not danger. I loved it when the sea acted like an unguent, a salve. And I loved it when I could hear music in the sea's movements.

Eventually, the Atlantic tied a leash around me, caught me in that viscous cocoon, that unctuous dream, that other plasma, so that I never wanted to let it out of touch or sight. I was infected, despite my sinuses beginning to fill and the bony growths in my ear kicking in. I gradually worked through a tough apprenticeship, not only of knowledge and skill, but also of attitude. I saw a few talents go awry through over-ripe egos. My heroes were the watermen and women, the ones who scanned the ocean carefully for its signs, who sacrificed time to paddling practice, who listened, and who surfed whatever the conditions, without complaint.

For me, control through style became the goal of surfing. I modelled this on a supposed conversation between bird and fish (or, strictly, mammal) – the equipoise of the hovering kestrel and the grace and playfulness of the dolphin, with its sudden bursts of power, and the balance between keeping the beat and improvising a solo that is central to jazz. I held the space between sea-life and bird-life, light like the bubble in the wash of waves, pulled by surface tension on that slight oil that is the water's membrane. The more I locked into that space between sky and water, gravity and levity, with confidence, the better the improvised solos. Control is poise and presence, not force or arrogance; poetics, not persuasion. I put in the hours, the months, the years, so that I was good enough to pick a set

Join the party – Nagpan, the Philippine.

wave at its earliest gasp, stay with the motion of the sump, and dialogue with it until its final sigh. I like to think of a session as a round – jump into the water off the sand, and complete the ride on the sand with a clean kick-out – the coda.

The satisfaction of performing to an audience, like a musician, pushed me to competition surfing. But I could only keep up the professional side of surfing because I had the antidote of travel and adventure, without the hassle of contest heats. I was fired up to study geography by a brilliant teacher, Barry Blamey. He packed more into one moment than many do in a lifetime. When I was at university, and trying to square this with a nascent career as an athlete, I felt at one point that I would have to give up my academic interests to follow surfing full time. But the postmodern world is about fluidity and multiple identities. Why not do both at once and see how they intertwine? Why not let one feed the other, so that both can push the boundaries and shift adaptation into innovation? I graduated from Cambridge University and successfully defended my European Longboard title. I am glad that I stuck with this dual choice, because I have been able to inform my surf travels and adventures with geographical knowledge, and this in turn is now leading to developing a career as a writer.

John Callahan and Masaai warrior – Lamu, Kenya

The earth – and the way that human cultures interact with her – fascinates me. As a geographer, I have put theory into practice through a deep love of travel. When I met the pioneering professional surf photographer John Callahan, he gave me the opportunity to take this yearning for discovery into cutting-edge work. John's speciality was to go to remote coastlines, often in Asia, Central America and Africa, where hardly anyone had photographed surfers riding the waves – Siargao in the Philippines, Anjouan in the Comoros, and Kumari Point in the Andaman Islands. Getting to the waves is a complex engagement, not just dropping off the side of the surf charter boat and paddling a couple of hundred metres to the break to ride another perfect hollow tube. Indeed, having sampled that, what the magazines do not tell you about are the hidden snags, such as having to queue for your spot in the line-up, only to find that just before take-off, a zodiac buzzing surfers back and forth to the break creates its own wake, that double-crosses the normally smooth face of the reef and throws you right out of kilter.

Improvisation is essential.

Jazz is all about improvisation. But 'jazz' is not just a kind of music – the primary African-American art form. It is a way of thinking and doing (around and under the beat). So surfers can be jazz players, without ever liking or knowing jazz, where they have that jazz feel for riding a wave that takes them away from the straight line and the standard moves. Thinking jazz is to live an improvised life, one in which imagination, not convention, is at the core.

The title-tune for Thelonious Monk's *Brilliant Corners* was so challenging, that, after 25 takes the band gave up. For the first time ever in a recording studio, the engineer cut the fragile tape with a razor blade and pasted it together with sticky tape, hence inventing by hand-and-eye the kind of cut-and-paste music that is now everyday and done electronically. Monk's album was that of an erratic genius who saw 'corners' not as dark spaces in which dust and spiders' webs gathered, but as angles of intent for a strange, dislocated modern jazz music that created space through timing and phrasing. Monk's 'corners' were curved.

Talented surfers think like Thelonious Monk, turning impossible wave scenarios into beautiful but challenging music. In shortboarding, Kelly Slater has absorbed the history of his sport and its key figures, from Michael Petersen to Tom Curren, to reinvent what is possible on a wave by 'thinking jazz' – thinking invention, spontaneity and 'brilliant corners'. No straight lines, no room for squares, but plenty of acute rebounds. Slater visited places on waves that were previously uncharted, and then joined the crew who left waves for aerial surfing with consummate ease. In longboarding and 'retro' surfing, Joel Tudor reinvented tradition, offering a new vocabulary of style that outfunked Thelonious Monk's strange chords and tinkling runs. Other surfers, such as Bonga Perkins, rolled up the entire history of graceful but powerful Hawaiian surfing, and let loose in free surfing and contest surfing in ways that showed an astonishing all-round capability. Laird Hamilton took his step-father, Billy Hamilton's, elegant style and added immense power and courage to tackle the world's most outrageous waves on creative equipment, pulling off the impossible.

My way of thinking jazz is to realize the brilliant corners of the world through extreme travel. By looking into the face of 'other' cultures, setting my dial to zero and reassessing what living is about, I am shaping an identity and a character. We often talk about 'lifestyle', but rarely about style in life. They are not the same. Forming an identity is about developing style, shaping oneself aesthetically and ethically – doing things that call up beauty, elegance and presence, but that are not at other people's expense, or, most importantly, at the expense of the planet. The message that runs through this book is heartfelt and simple: it is about developing poise as a person, and about caring for the planet as a collective. We are in a deep ecological crisis, and I do not want to pass on that dreadful legacy to

Overleaf: Journey to the centre of the earth – El Nido, the Philippine

Above: Solo runs – Kumari Point, Andaman Islar
Left: Eagle's view – with Icah Wilmont and Zed Layson, mountaintop fortress, Ha

future generations. We have to act in considerate ways, and this means facing major conundrums. If I love to travel and that is part of my lifeblood, how do I square that with the terrible environmental effects of long-haul flights? I do not yet have a good answer to this, but I do not want to brush it under the carpet.

While Robinson Crusoe was horrified to discover the footprint of another on 'his' island, I try to walk carefully in the footsteps of the local inhabitants, to know what it is like to live in those places in which we are, strictly, itinerant surf tourists. I prefer to think the sea and travel shape me, rather than imagining that I stamp my identity on anything. This book is about the footsteps I have followed – those of inspiring travellers, surfers and photographers; and about the footprints that I, and others, may have left as we travelled to surf. By approaching new situations with an openness and a willingness to learn, I have come to appreciate that there is a place between acceptance and confidence that, again, demands poise. All surfers know the feeling of poise. The trick is how you translate that moment into life as a whole, sustaining poise. Once in this more receptive, open mindset, a magic session comes when I least expect it. It carves a smile on my face, keeping my fires stoked until another sunset tips whole into a plum-coloured sea and I am the only one left surfing under a rising moon, still stoked, already planning the dawn patrol. Beyond the wave, I have stood on spectacular Middle Eastern desert dunes that rumble like thunder as they shift underfoot; I have paddled through brown Asian rivermouths with dangerous, saw-dentured water-life tracking my shadow; I have openly defied the law in a law-abiding country to ride a heart-pounding typhoon swell in South Korea; and driven through African war-torn border patrols, wondering if I have the right papers, already planning the weight of the bribe, and sometimes wondering whether a trigger-happy soldier might just reduce this trip, this life to a zero.

2 Haitian Fight Song

In Cap-Haïtien, shutters hang on rusty hinges. Doors creak in Creole. Balconies crumble, and colour wash fades and peels, in a last gasp of colonial grandeur. Haiti's bright paint has never properly washed out. It is set by the deep stain of history. I am privileged to draw this in through my senses without fear, as one of the first visitors in years to walk around this town not threatened by violence. Le Cap used to be described by visitors as 'Little Paris' and 'The Pearl of the Antilles'. Her charm persists, experienced as a vibrant ebb and flow of life across a thin barrier. Haiti hangs between chaos and control, making the heart race, but also capturing that heart like an unpredictable lover.

Locals step elegantly over steaming piles of trash, goods balanced delicately on their heads, weaving past wheelbarrows selling everything from dental floss to dinner jackets. There is a raw competition for space measured in output of sweat on a deeply hot day. A basket overflowing with bicycle parts is roughly pulled aside to allow the easy passage of a huge barrow laden with ice. Perspiration flows down the hauler's back, echoing the speed of the ice-melt. A tottering pig squeals, and is strapped back into a pushcart plump with fresh plantains.

Mobile pharmacies advertise their medicines for sale through loud hailers, obviating the need for street drugs. This is no pre-modern Haitian market but a postmodern carnival. The informal economy is thriving. Someone zigzags through the mayhem on a motorbike with a highly explosive acetylene cylinder slung over his shoulder. He bumps, wobbles, nearly loses it, tweaks the accelerator, speeds on and rebalances – seemingly oblivious to the fact that he is dynamite on wheels. Cliff-hangers pop up everywhere – rickety old pick-ups transformed into 'tap-taps' thread through the crowds, pull in close to curb sides to pick up and drop off passengers, and pull out just as swiftly, without ever seeming to collide. The tap-taps are richly decorated, tattooed all over in holy signs, unholy marriages of ancient icons and advertising hoardings, praising *Dieu* and *Don Jesus, Jesus Roi des Rois,* and *Dieu avant tous*. The vehicle – in fact the flux of street life itself – is blessed by these icons; a fatal accident never seems to happen. Instead there is a weave with an absent weaver, a collection of knots with no centre that holds. Yet death – perhaps the absent weaver, the heart of the knot-work – is everywhere, waiting in the wings. In the syncretic Catholic-Voodoo view, one must live dangerously, close to death, and invite the dead into the place of the living as a preparation for the afterlife. Alive and kicking, groups of smiling children walk by in colourful school uniforms – blue ribbons for one class, pink for another. Laundered clothes are dried on dusty cacti. The skeleton is coaxed out, up front, scrubbed clean and worn on the outside. Expect reversal in Haiti. Those kids are death's messengers – from birth we are born to die, and so must make a relationship with death, an early pact. A Haitian proverb says '*Après dans tanbou lou*' – 'After the dance, the drum is heavy.'

Haiti can be heavy – blue-black – her body already bruised from history. But her skeleton is a pearl, rubbed to hard brilliance from grit. In the right place at the right intensity, her bones seem to sing. Your bones rattle back. Haiti gets under your skin. This is the antithesis to the easygoing, rum-shack stereotype. Closer to West Africa in mood, the Cap-Haïtien coast is a darker prospect than the transparent

Life, death and the place in between – Cap Haïtien

First sight of surfing – Cap Haïtien coast

body of the Caribbean. History tells us why: these were the first people to successfully challenge slavery. Those beaten skins and grim ghost solos linger from the drums of history.

Exhausted by the tension, yet exhilarated by this living in, or between, two worlds, we head out of town, west along the north coast. Zed Layson, a close friend from Barbados, with a big reputation, is the quickest to his feet on our first surf in Haiti. He pushes deep into the skin of the wave, and as he bends it in snaking turns, small splits appear where shavings of bones show as fans of spray. A group of locals lines the shore, hair stiffened by charcoal smoke, garments torn by the rough sandstone, palms slippery from fish scales. Live fire coral pokes through the wave face, but Zed races over the hot skeleton, avoiding the danger, and kicks out. From land, photographer John Callahan captures the angles with a striking frame, turning the moment into the eternal, getting under the skin of the action.

I catch the next wave, getting high on the nose, up near the lip, to avoid touching any live wires just beneath the sea's skin. A long, stretching ride brings the audience to a common chorus of wild support, like fanning hot coals to suddenly bring the flame back from near death. As I kick out, a girl on the shore breaks into a shakedown. Maybe an aspiring *Vodouisant*, her gyrations beat by a distance anything that Zed has seen in two decades of Sunday's 'shake-yer-booty contest' in Barbados – and that is some contest. 'And that is some dancing,' says Zed, contemplating a scrape on the reef on his second wave as his attention is diverted. The heavy drumbeat is there, in the background, always in the background. We are all in a skeleton dance, walking a fine line, a paradoxical fire-line hanging just below the water, calculating the risks, and, as surfers do, testing the limits, getting the rhythm.

This wave is just at the edge of chaos. One slip and your skin is sloughed, your bones ready to show. Even the smallest contact with those electric coral heads will cut, and without quick treatment an infected wound follows. To keep balance you have to move at speed. In Haiti you live life with intensity – maximum complexity this side of the curtain. But do not go over to the side of chaos unless your life is already at low ebb – best invite death on to your side for conversation and rehearsal. Be prepared for the deadly intensity of that conversation. Rehearse. For me, rehearsal comes with travel to what, for others, may be the backwaters of the world, but these are the brilliant corners – places that have just emerged from conflict, or have shunned conventional tourism. Our backwater is somebody's home and ancestral ground, their front yard. In Haiti, we soon find that reversal of view is a way of life.

Why do flocks of birds not clatter into each other when they swoop and wheel? Watch for the patterns – each bird need only sense the movement of the nearest two, and this spreads throughout the flock, maintaining the shape. In Cap-Haïtien people move in seemingly chaotic swarms, but nobody seems to collide. No 'teams' here – an industrial notion – but teeming, swarming, meshing, knot-working. Haitians have an added, complicating dimension – the unpredictable movement of the unseen spirit realm. A tangled rhizomatic structure underpins what you see, like fungal webs living symbiotically with the roots of trees, from which the reproductive structures – mushrooms – occasionally pop up and release their spores. At any moment, the spirit web might mischievously undo your life assemblage – an accident of nature. It is clear from the street life here that the spirits inhabit busy places, choose to crush into the smallest spaces, so that they fizz and bustle. Conversation with them will turn you inside out, just like the live coral-reef slough and its awkward present of infection. I survive that first hectic surf without hitting the reef. But those crowded spirits are also your best cure for the ordinary. When they effervesce and agitate and your feet get itchy for new shores, expect the extraordinary.

Overleaf: Rastaman Icah Wilmont visiting Haiti from Jamaic

At Cormier Plage we are the first tourists in a long time. My oldest friend from Cornwall, Tristan Jenkin, an excellent shortboarder, is part of our travelling band. He asks the waitress for a banana in what I think is pretty good French. She comes out of the kitchen with a pool cue. No matter how polished your French, Haitian Creole is more complicated, more below-ground. The sugary shaddock grapefruit refuels us and we have the energy for another long surf. Ginsu is a short walk. This spot is spirited, double-edged – if the serrated lip doesn't catch you, the razor reef will. As we play out a session the glassy waves curve, bowl and roll following a simple bass theme, easy to hum, like the opening to jazz legend Charles Mingus' 'Haitian Fight Song'. But a few sets in and the session becomes more complex. We choose to make it more complex, increasingly taking risks, our awareness more tuned in to how close we can get to the 'chopping board' rock on the inside.

Mingus, the great American jazz composer, bandleader and bassist, wrote 'Haitian Fight Song' for the album *The Clown*, to imitate the intense lives of the Haitian people he so admired, and to protest against the legacy of slavery. From its slow and even pulse, the tune builds and swings, finally into a wail that reflects the Haitians' intense resolution and desire to live life to the maximum, abandoning easy, sweet melody for complex engagement. Throughout, what is beautiful about this track is the tone – slightly and purposefully off the register, as if a weight has to be borne, or a tug from another world is always felt.

Meanwhile, I am unpacking my own symbols, with trademark, high-in-the-lip noserides, neat footwork, a swooping roundhouse cut-back and a full, arcing bottom turn to skitter across the fraying lip, hook back, and then drop into the slot at full speed for a freight-train run under the falling curtain – a quick cover-up – and then a fade and once more a high cross-step to the nose, this time poised enough to hang all ten toes over the tip, an arch, some nimble footwork back to the tail and a reverse kick-out, a backhand exit. This round of symbols is a repertoire, a ceremony, a faithfully enacted drama, a gig. The board is my instrument. But the wave has better chops than me. It will blow me off stage every time. See how each wave's melody rolls out in long, unique and sinuous lines, how the piano player suddenly snaps into double time as the wave folds ahead. How will I respond? Read the wave down the line. Set up ahead of time. Syncopation is essential, but this time anticipating the beat and playing just in front of it, then lagging slightly, purposefully, to create that open, cool sound.

Tentacles protrude from shallow cores, bright yellow-green and brown stingers everywhere. It is the shallowest wave I have ever ridden – a Voodoo lesson in living dangerously. In the close-clipped field at the foot of the headland, overlooking the surf, locals gather for a ritual, dressed in white. They venerate a pantheon of Catholic saints as a web of personified Voodoo spirits grounded in the exportation of

Left: Bajan Zed Layson taking an early shower, and curtain razors – Ginsu

African religious beliefs through the slave trade. In a materially poor community, a rich spiritual life is vital. Voodoo touches all Haitians because it values family bonds, community interests and care for those who are worse off. Singing and dancing are ways of shaking away the bonds to earthly life and slipping into a spirit world, temporarily, as a sinister rinse for deepening life, and a preparation for death. There is a thin and permeable curtain between this world and the otherworld that can be crossed in ecstasy and possession. The singing becomes a loud, vibrating chorus. Knowledge of the dead can be brought back to animate this life. We watch and listen from the unusual perspective of the surfer looking back to land. The sound is now stunning, pulsating and resonating off the hills, gathering intense flavour in the journey. Voodoo promises risk in such spirit conversations, but the great gift is that of being in rhythm and tone, of inhabiting the pulse of events so that you live elegantly, like those pure notes dripping from Miles Davis' trumpet.

Voodoo allows you to 'see through' things – to see through the lens of animal life getting close to nature, and to see through the follies of humanity. But there can be slippage, the danger of possession leading to madness or death. Wearing the skeleton on the outside of the body, as inversion, says that you accept that life sits with death. Put up your hand and say, honestly, 'I am scared.' Only the foolish and the vain would aim for immortality. 'Seeing the skeleton' is the central vision of shamanism, which is to allow life to rattle your bones. Voodoo is a risky business, as is life. Rhythm is a risky business, as is tone – nobody likes a bum note, a blue note that turns sour, or a honeyed note that is too sickly, and there is nothing that offends the spirits more than those who pretend rhythm but cannot keep time. Voodoo says: care for a friend, love your children, share your food with the needy and always walk the line, even where the roots rise to tangle your steps.

The singing stops, I catch a wave, the curtain falls, I wipeout. The fire coral scrapes my skin with a raking burn. Curtain razors for a split-second drama, sharp as hell. Spirit fires. My bones sing out in the subsequent clatter and bounce. We all take a hit on this session. The light is golden before the sun slips behind the Bonnet mountains, as I paddle ringside, over the urchin forest, scuffing the board to save another stinging scrape. I duck through the salt-stained foliage and past the place where the ceremony happened, where the notes were true and still hang in the air. The walk back to Cormier Plage along a twisting limestone road adds to its smooth wear, the stone now like marble, past the bearded goats and plump pigs, to the small village where the men play dominoes, the loser covered in clothes pegs as ritual humiliation. Prize cocks relax for the fight on Sunday where winner takes all. A United Nations (UN) tank roars past, packed with bored Chilean patrol troops who have nothing to do but stir a grass snake to activity. The local fishermen, however, are busy, breaking up a wrecked boat to reclaim the wood for building. Hard wood is met by hard work, and matched by worksong, the Creole chorus helping to ease the strain: 'Men anpil chay pa lou' – 'Many hands make the load lighter.'

Place your deposits, and prize fighter – Cap Haïtie

The sky turns banana-beige, then charcoal, and sparks fly from cooking pits. The spirits sit around and talk. They discuss how slaves gained control of a country in an uprising, reversing the sinister order of twisted authority, and vowed to reverse sensation, by wearing their nervous systems on the outside so that they would always be on guard, alert to the awful refrain of the master's voice. They formed a nation and further agreed that they would never harbour greed. 'The giver of the blow forgets, the bearer of the scar remembers,' they say. Haiti was born wild, and has remained so in the face of nervous and needy capitalists. But there is no poverty of spirit here.

In its everyday show of surface tension, Haiti is like a breaking wave. The blue face curls into white eddies over a bed of coral – a glowing skeleton and an itching phosphor, underwater rhizomes. In the wrong spot, you will get hurt. In the pocket, with momentum, you will sing in tone and rhythm. But you have to take the leap with courage, face the taboo in the Voodoo. On an extreme surf trip, it takes a bit of grit to make a pearl. I kept my balance the best I could, got great waves and got skinned, dancing with the spirits with whom I have best communion – those of the sea. I am honoured to be a band member. I am grateful for getting hooked on surfing all those years ago. Peering out from the window of the plane as I leave Port-au-Prince, heading home to Cornwall, I recall another Haitian proverb that has lodged in my mind: 'Dèyè mòn gen mòn' – 'Behind mountains there are more mountains.' Under the skin, the skeleton calls. Do you recognize the tune?

3 The Birth of Cool

I remember the pungent smell of kelp drawn out by a searing Californian sun as I waded into the pebble-bottom shallows at San Onofre. I turned my head to shore. The morning fog had wholly burned off, and Dad's face lit up. Fellow Cornishman and close family friend Paul Holmes had lent me a sparkling channel-bottomed, Hawaiian-shaped shortboard. To me, a gangly kid, it was perfectly crafted, instilling a wonderful self-confidence. Paul was the then editor of *Surfer* magazine, considered 'the Bible of the sport'. He had an injured shoulder from a trip to Bali, and watched from the beach. Outback, Dad and I shared the ocean with pelicans and a host of locals. I saw the thick frown of an approaching set spoil the otherwise calm skin of the sea, paddled out towards it, swung back around and stroked into that wave alone. It peaked, turned green and, as it broke, I took off, angled and found trim. Groomed by the kelp and cobbles, the wave unfurled further than I could see. Light bounced back off the face, which turned to a wet glare. I rode its entire length, locked in the pocket. The feathering frown had become a big smile, Hollywood-style, white teeth showing. Dad and Paul hooted proudly. That wave was a defining moment – I was finally a surfer.

Before the family spent a year in the USA in the 1980s, surfing was a duet, my dad pushing me safely into Cornwall's cool-water waves. At sun-bleached San Onofre, I finally went solo, paddling out beyond the whitewater and completing the whole cycle with proper trim. Paul gave me the board, and back home in West Penwith I was set up for life. I got the hang of it – catching waves, standing up in one smooth movement, turning, kicking out. Dad helped me to not develop bad habits, like getting up on one knee first – spring to your feet in one go – and to try to complete a ride with a clean kick-out. From the unpredictability of the surf I learned adaptability – to smell the fast-changing weather coming and going, to feel the beat of the moon's influence through big tidal changes. Most importantly, I learned how to read the sea and use the rip currents. And only on the Celtic fringe could you be chased by a bullock in your dew-lagged wetsuit, launch over a granite hedge, slip and fall on to the electric cattle fence and into a bed of stinging nettles, then tumble down spectacular sand dunes to an orchestra of skylarks, to recover in a pounding beachbreak.

My appreciation for Cornish surf slipped up a notch on a clear autumn morning when there was a big swell running with a light offshore wind, and we ventured out at a rocky reef. There was a great lefthander working from the boil on the outside rock, where the seals hang out. The paddle out was eerie – seaweed-

Photo: Greg Martin

Local playground – West Penwith , Cornwall

strewn, slate grey – and I went cautiously, lingering behind Dad. A good set came through, and he caught a cracker. I floundered around on the inside. Finally in position, I turned for a wave. It doubled up and surged dramatically, snagging me on take-off. I steamed shoreward until I felt the fins clip against the stringy seaweed, and slipped in the oily tangle. I was dragged through the dark descent of the undertow. I came up gasping for air, etched with relief, but full of life. We were the only ones out at a spot that was working perfectly; there was a beautiful tang of seaweed in the air, a little uncertainty because the peak is right over a rock that you can practically stand on as the set sweeps in, and more than a little mystery. I overcame some fear that day, and when I paddled in I felt that I had properly caught the buzz of surfing.

Days later I met another local young surfer, Tristan Jenkin. We were in the sea as much as possible, surfing and bodysurfing at Gwenver, Sennen and Perranuthnoe, before 'tombstoning' off rocks at high tide and crashing on the beach, exhausted, wind-chapped and wiped out from sunburn. Like many other surfers around the world, our resonance with the glory years of Californian surf culture was shaped by John Milius' cult film *Big Wednesday*. It uses the seasons as a

Reality meets the legend – Malibu, California

metaphor for changes in life, not only of its main characters but also of American culture, through the golden 1960s longboard era, the Vietnam years, and ending with the dominance of the shortboard and Hawaii as the epicentre. The climax is the 'great swell' that reunites the boys for a tear-jerker scene for men. They put aside old differences to paddle out together to encounter the once-in-a-lifetime surf. This is where they will all 'eat it', but not before each has a moment of glory. Heroism is grounded in finding kinship through a common love of the sea. You will not find *Big Wednesday* on the list of all-time great movies (Milius had already achieved that with his script for *Apocalypse Now*). Indeed, the film bombed in America, but was a huge hit in Italy, the home of style. It is based on Malibu surf lore – the crucible of post-war performance longboarding in California – and made as homage to the time Milius spent there during his youth.

After the Second World War, two powerful cultural events emerged in America. In New York, modern jazz – 'bebop' – was born, replacing swing music in popularity, and generating a whole new way of phrasing, with an emphasis upon syncopation and improvisation. In California wave-riding expertise exploded with the development of aerospace-inspired foam and fibreglass surfboards – cheaper and lighter than the cumbersome redwood and balsa planks that went before. Malibu offered a predictable ride along a long cobble point, ideal for the development of a smooth 'hotdogging' repertoire that many surfers still crave. Turning from the tail, 'shooting the curl' and 'walking the nose' was eloquently modelled by Phil Edwards. Later this style was re-enacted in *Big Wednesday* by Billy Hamilton in the role of surf star and 'hot local', Matt – casual, confident and intense. The 'Malibu' boards were provocative instruments for the collective imagination of a new wave of surfers, none of whom could have possibly envisaged a second wave of design change in the late 1960s, where boards shrank from 10-foot 'logs' to head-high 'sticks', mirroring design in guitar bodies. And through the changing lengths the best surfers, from hotdogger Billy Hamilton to tubemaster Gerry Lopez, played their boards like jazz musicians blew their horns, with style and improvisation.

Surfing was associated with sun-filled days, the Californian love of leisure and health, the wide, open lung of the Pacific breathing life into a post-war genera-tion. Jazz was moon music, played under naked bulbs in smoke-filled bars late at night. And modern jazz was the most demanding, intensive and engaging of art forms, dependent on sustained improvisation and exquisite timing. When bebop got so fast and frantic it became unplayable unless you were technically brilliant, Miles Davis started to leave spaces in his music – the 'birth of cool' – to allow phrases to hover and hangout with casual intensity. Jazz broadcast inven-tion across city radio waves. Jazz was cool. Jazzlife hipsters and beats were arbiters of fashion – berets, horn-rimmed glasses, polonecks and tight jeans for beats; and for hipsters, sharp Italian suits, Brooks Brothers button-down-collar shirts with skinny ties, Bass Weejun loafers, and just-below-the-knee black pencil dresses. *Cool Struttin'* exclaimed the title of pianist Sonny Clark's 1958 Blue Note label album. The tenor saxophonist Hank Mobley put it another way with his 1963 album title *No Room for Squares*. A stalwart of the legendary Blue Note label, Hank Mobley was one of the best stylists in modern jazz, playing around the beat to create space. A blue note was an imaginatively squashed note, played with soul – a note that oozed quality and feeling, and signalled 'style'.

1960s California surfing style was smooth and seamless, drawing a tight line, leaving a feather trace. There is sometimes depth in surfaces. The West coast offered a step over the final frontier towards the place of the setting sun, into the Pacific, signifying a new freedom and a rogue identity. Where the mainstream embraced the Hollywood myth of eternal daylight, by never wanting to drop into the underworld with the setting sun – and then became a cosmetic culture – surf-ers were prepared to take the drop. Their collective initiation was the 'wipeout'. They craved adventure and danger, to tame the dangerous Pacific and remain on the fringe. Surfers were outsiders, agitators, who somehow knew instinctively the rules of nature and could openly call themselves 'royalty', following what was pre-

One of the goals – hanging ten at Sennen, Cornwall

served for kings and queens in Polynesia. Appropriated elements of Polynesian culture were made 'cool', and surfing soon became popular and commercialized, with a labour-intensive industry, using environmentally toxic materials, developing as the dark side feeding the light freedoms of 'hanging ten'.

My dad, Paul Holmes, and many others, soaked up both the American jazz and exported surf fever in Cornwall in the 1960s. By the early 1970s, they were running a cutting-edge 'alternative' newspaper, the first serious surf journalism in Britain – *Surf Insight* – offering lucid comment on political, social and environmental issues. *Surf Insight* was ahead of its time, making surfing an intellectual as well as a physical and emotional adventure. For Paul it was an apprenticeship that would get him right to the top of the surf-journalism ladder, first editing *Tracks* magazine in Australia, and then *Surfer* in America. For Dad, surfing in Cornwall has remained a constant companion through his academic career and his love of jazz music.

Growing up in Cornwall, I cherished not only the land, sea and wildlife, but also the different atmospheres, the sudden weather changes. You mark out some of these as particularly special, like those rare times when the sea is shrouded with vapour from a rowdy swell, and the smell mixes with that of damp earth rising from the land. This place is still for me the end of the earth – in summer bathed in reflected light from the ocean; in winter, stark, sinister and bleak. The changes are extreme and extraordinary; the air is pure, and the light reflects from the sea to give clarity and colour that are hard to match. At night, there is no light pollution and the stars are spectacular. The lows, or depressions, bring surf, but also mirrored moods, the Atlantic weather sweeping up and down the leg of Britain as if an agitated giant were rolling and unrolling a sock of mist and rain.

West Penwith is at the toe of the foot of Cornwall, perched on a massive upwelling of granite. At the rugged north-west edge igneous rock bursts through the hills, exposing high cliffs hovering over windswept beaches. The southerly underbelly is lush, with sheltered evergreen woods bisected by turbulent streams that run away to feed the sea. The further west one goes, the more concentrated are the Neolithic burial sites, culminating in the Isles of Scilly. This makes sense, as the sun sets here and is reborn on the opposite horizon. The dead must surely follow the sun, as it is dissolved daily only to rise elsewhere. Here, the Southern Californian dream of reclaiming the sun before it drops, of maintaining a permanent Hollywood smile and persona, was never going to catch on in the same way. The locals drop with the sun and suffer the consequences as winter depressions grip. Indeed, the initiation is vital. Months with short days and yeasty rain can turn you to California Dreaming.

After studying *Big Wednesday* religiously, my greatest hope in surfing was to become a 'hot local'. It is corny, comic-book stuff, but the film captures the essence of the Malibu mindset – a unique relationship between dream, desire and place, where the more you step in, the more you stand out. *Big Wednesday* made me want desperately to go surfing, so when longboards began making an unexpected return to line-ups – as a recovery of style response to the radical slash-and-burn shortboard era – I was desperate to get involved.

By the 1990s, postmodern surfing embraced punk-infused, aerial-infested shortboarding, back-to-the-roots longboarding and everything in between. While I learned on shortboards, I was soon drawn to surfing's retro revival made 'cool' by a long-haired pre-teen Californian prodigy named Joel Tudor. Riding lightweight versions of older style boards, Joel Tudor, and the evergreen Hawaiian Bonga Perkins, who could surf any size with consummate ease, had the talent and bravado to combine historical references from the 1960s with a unique, futuristic approach clearly influenced by shortboard carving. They, and a handful of others, particularly American Herbie Fletcher, Australian Nat Young and Hawaiian Rusty Keaulana, formed a bridge between the past and future that was hugely influential.

Cornwall's first-generation surf stars – Dad's good friends and guiding lights for me – Roger Mansfield and Chris Jones, were at the forefront of the rising tide of Britain's longboarding renaissance. When Dad and I got hold of a neon-sprayed modern featherweight longboard, I paddled out charged with excitement. There was a low ceiling of cloud that looked more like dark smoke, hovering over a heron-blue sea that at one moment was eerily calm, and the next, riddled with activity as seven-wave sets, wedging into powerful A-frames, raced to hurl themselves at the beach. There was already a good crowd out, scratching for position, some cutting and slashing, others flailing and falling. The rights were breaking at a really high tempo, like a pianist making a run, a frantic solo, culminating in a succession of crashing chords as the shorebreak's coda. This was familiar, if complex, music. The seabirds knew it intimately, as they rose and fell against the bass-line of the swell and then took solo runs gliding close to the feathering edge of the waves. Turning to take the third wave of a set, I sprang to my feet, and sensed such board control I was sure I could learn to improvise to the sea's pulse in a fluid and inventive style. This was the moment I discovered the obvious – how strongly surfing style is influenced by the conversation between board, body and wave, and how often surfers, especially those who have just mastered the essentials, attempt to force this conversation. Sunlight pierced the clouds and I was so energized that I surfed for five hours under that clearing sky until dusk drew in.

The following day the conditions were abysmal – small waves, with a gusty cross-shore wind and a slack tide. I was hungry to try the board again and slid left on a steel grey section, swung right, and before I could even admire the way the board found that rare gem of clean face, I was gingerly cross-stepping up to the nose as if cognitively programmed from watching *Big Wednesday*. The moment my toes curled around the tip, a blaze of energy penetrated my core. Some neural network had settled and meshed. The feeling of poise was addictive. The noseride, for me, became the defining aspect of longboarding, but then all I was doing was recapitulating the history of surfing. I felt that history unwinding like a genie released from the lamp. I wanted to study the moves of the great longboarders, and then develop my own style. The local crew thought I had sold out. I was the only young longboarder in the line-up. But my dad, his first-generation surf friends, and what was happening in brilliant corners of California, Hawaii and Australia, spurred me on. I knew I was tuning into something interesting.

I devoured every frame of every surfing video I could get my hands on. I watched every nuance in style – old, new, short and long. I liked the videos that did not feature amazing conditions, but amazing surfers doing impossible things on the kinds of waves I surfed at home. I felt that if I studied the moves, I could learn to do them. I started to bring better timing and torque into conversation riding shortboards, but it was longboarding that induced a new kind of stoke, and gave me a way to combine tradition with progression.

The hang ten remained elusive, until the first autumn long-distance groundswell swept in and the beach was strewn in heaped ribbons of dank seaweed.

Right and overleaf: Learning the longboard dance –
hang five, hang ten and cutback – in the Philippines

I knee-paddled out to glaucous green water, with delicate foam lines raking around and beyond Aire Point at Gwenver's own brilliant corner. A cormorant bobbed up beside me and then dived, showing how duck-diving should be done. I took off, arced into a long bottom turn, pulled up high in the curl and walked to the nose. My confidence was now fully ripe. I could spot a slowing section, and was beginning to link visualization with body movement to read the wave ahead of time. I stepped forward and hung ten, wringing out a bright, lingering sound. Apply weight, remaining weightless: the Zen paradox of noseriding. Some things are about intensity and quality, not longevity. The moment was so packed it seemed to expand and happen in slow motion – the experience you also get in the tube. That paradox, I knew, would carry me through my surfing life. I felt like a hot coal in a rainstorm – a short and spectacular Charlie Parker saxophone solo. I could hear hoots from the crowd behind. They were convinced.

The biggest surf wear company of the 1960s, Hang Ten, based in California, showed two bare feet as its trademark, and it became a symbol of surfing. Thirty years later, all surfers knew the semiotics – ten toes over. Like a tuberide or aerial, it still raises a cheer of respect. In Cornwall, I could not claim San Onofre, a Californian climate, or long right pointbreaks like Malibu, but I certainly started to cherish an imported, and then home-grown, longboard 'cool'.

Jazz musicians invented cool – hipsters, the beat generation. You were either hip or square. You've either got chops or you don't. 'Chops' is bottom-line musical ability and understanding that comes with practice and timing. Riding waves is all about timing. The best moves are syncopated, just behind the beat of the wave. This creates a space between the wave's time and the surfer's time that makes things interesting. Marching to the beat, military-style, is for squares, cool is to play slightly off the beat. I wanted to surf just as great jazz musicians blow – keeping in the pocket just off the beat. This is to not state the obvious, but to hint, with a sideways glance; to offer subtle intonations, or aching silences punctuated by perfectly timed clusters of notes. Or, best of all, to hit just a single shimmering blue note suspended in space by walking to the nose, and hanging ten, in perfect poise.

While there are many styles of jazz, they all embody rhythm, timing, and above all, improvisation. The jazz musician, like the good surfer, is able to improvise around a melody or a set of chord changes. The oldest joke in music is: 'Can you tell me how to get to Carnegie Hall?' Answer: 'Practise! Practise!' Without your basics in place, improvisation is impossible. I had established the basics, the chords, and then set to work on my improvised lines against the ocean's shifting backdrop of bass and drums. In some music there is little room for improvisation – you play the written score, or stick to a winning formula, a predictable

Right: Hovering behind the beat – South Korea
The floater – the Maldives

chord sequence. But jazz and surfing are nothing without improvisation. I did not want to just read music and stick to the score, or only imitate the path-breakers. I wanted to get at what Thelonious Monk called the 'brilliant corners' of improvised music – the title of one of the most extraordinary albums in modern music.

The 1940s experimentation in jazz led by the later work of Ike Quebec, Thelonius Monk, Charlie 'Yardbird' Parker, Max Roach, Charles Mingus, Bud Powell and Dizzy Gillespie, that was 'bebop' – characterized by double-time, frantic solos – settled into 'post-bop', and the music started to feel comfortable. Good musicians were seen as imitators of the innovators. Bop began to fade, and something new was needed. Miles Davis felt that bop had lost space. It was too frantic, too packed. Light needed to enter the density, which was like a tidal wave at times. Miles wanted to bring music in through the back door to sneak up quietly on the listener and snatch his or her heart. Stealth, extraordinary beauty, elegance – these were not in the furious double and triple times of bebop, which in the hands of the masters was magnificent, but grated in the hands of the imitators.

In the 1950s, Miles Davis was joined particularly by West Coast musicians Gerry Mulligan, Chet Baker and Art Pepper, and arranger Gil Evans, to open up jazz through creating space, languid phrasing and luminous, lingering notes. The 'birth of cool' turned frantic acoustic bop inside out, to release its space. This gave great emphasis to tone and vibrato, overshadowing clusters and runs of notes at triple time. On a longboard I learned to achieve space on the wave by slowing everything down, playing at half tempo, with good timing, to get at those all-important pauses. It made my surfing smoother. I could move around the beat by cross-stepping on the board and hover and hang higher-in-the-lip on the nose by soul arching, or raising my back arm. This is precisely how younger musicians get to copy the licks of the masters – they play a tough passage at a much slower tempo, getting into the notes and around the phrasing. And gradually, they build the tempo. Then they start to bend the original, try an inversion, subvert the melody, deliberately skipping notes to create an interesting space.

The real work comes when the soloist plays with the band, because now you have to work with and around others. My surfing got syncopated through careful opening of space around the wave's motion, using walking to create balance points to hang just behind or ahead of the beat, manoeuvring to create speed, then taking my foot on and off the accelerator entirely through trim created by subtle use of the rails. Remember the quartet. You cannot simply be a good soloist. You have to know what the other band members are up to. And I also had to remember that each one – the sea's moods, the swell's sudden shifts, the wind's intensity and the mobile sand bottom creating new channels – was more powerful, complex and infinitely more interesting than my crude balancing on a piece of foam and fibreglass.

When 1960s *avant-garde* players, inspired by black politics and angry at self-satisfied music that they saw as regressing to cocktail jazz, ripped up these 1950s forms, they reinvented the music as a 'fire music', as Archie Shepp called it. They purposefully played out of time and against the normal rules of harmony and ensemble, as 'free jazz'. They saw this as a replay of the agonies of slavery and the paradox of so-called 'freedom' for blacks in a white country. While a lot of this moved at breakneck speed, and much of it now sounds like cacophony, again what worked was the timing, the subtle pauses and space created within the music, whatever the tempo, by syncopation. This experimentation, led by John Coltrane, Archie Shepp, Ornette Coleman, Cecil Taylor, Don Cherry and others, left players like Miles Davis cold because he could not see beauty in the music. As much as anyone, Miles was incensed by the way that black people were treated in America, and was bowled over by the lack of prejudice when he visited Paris to play. But for Miles, black pride was pride in a particular kind of elegance, not a grunt or an overblow, an angry honk.

Miles Davis was always the experimenter, and listening closely in the 1960s to what was happening in rock music, he reinvented his music in the 1970s as electric jazz and 'fusion' – harmonic and melodic trumpet and saxophone lines meandering over heavy rock bass, drums, guitar and electric piano. Lyrical, heavyweight jazz musicians such as the saxophonist Wayne Shorter simply gave up what they had been doing for years, and invented a new kind of jazz form underpinned by the principles of rock music. The soprano rather than the tenor sax seemed to be a more natural solo voice, maintaining the deeply lyrical sound good players sought. For Miles, his *life* was jazz, played out like jazz – the clothes, the attitude, the pride in being black, the footwork of the boxer. When he played concerts, after his solos he would often turn his back on the audience, or just wander off. Some saw this as arrogance… but why hang around once the job is done?

By the end of the 1970s, people thought there was nothing left to do in jazz. No more paths to furrow. No more invention. But this is where the improvisers can step in. Great surfers and great musicians can take this history and reinvent it, refine it, bend it and even restore some of its forgotten corners. Something wonderful emerges. Ornette Coleman brought 'world' music influences into his 'harmolodics', and jazz felt young again. John Coltrane studied Indian music, and adopted some of its forms. Players like David Murray and Bill Frisell not only absorbed the entire history of the tenor saxophone and guitar, respectively, but demonstrated jaw-dropping technique through an openness to eclecticism. And this is surely the key for surfing – the likes of Kelly Slater, Laird Hamilton, Joel Tudor and Bonga Perkins have immaculate technique, exquisite timing – back to 'chops'. On top of this, they can reinvent the history of wave-riding because they are in a position to improvise and then mix it up in an eclectic way, drawing on the best of everything. Their styles speak the history of effortless surfing embodied in

Phil Edwards, Mickey 'Da Cat' Dora, David Nuuhiwa, Nat Young, Gerry Lopez, Larry Bertleman and Tom Curren. Not just a fusion of styles, but a recreation of tradition. And just as people catch on, they are already downstream, finding a new line.

Considering the surfing greats more as sources of inspiration than acts to copy, I pushed myself by putting on a performance where the beach area became a stage – actor and critic. It was a regulated self-display, a way of 'giving off', just as birdsong is mostly non-functional, but for sheer expression, the joy of singing, the majesty of sound. Not about territory, or finding a mate, but just for the sake of the display. Is this frivolous? Not at all – it is the basic motivation for any art form. 'Eighty per cent of bird song is non-functional' was one of Mum's art exhibition titles (she is a sculptor and painter), reminding us that the world is first and foremost an expression, an aesthetic event. Beauty needs to be appreciated before it is explained. The point of a life is to use one's senses, to listen and notice things closely – an aesthetic adventure. And jazz is a great metaphor to frame this.

What I enjoyed from music as applied to surfing was not just improvisation and syncopation, but, fundamentally, rhythm. Where good surfers improvise through extended syncopation, knowing how to match the uncertainty of the wave's motion, it is rhythm that keeps all of this together. Without a sense of rhythm, surfers look awkward, unsure and unstable. But rhythm is not just about riding the wave with great timing, it is about the art and style of the whole surfing experience: eyeing the conditions, judging where to paddle out, duck diving, finding the take-off spot and exploring its limits. The complete ride, as one round performance, is from paddle-in to kick-out, often in a crowd. This is a holistic grasp of a gig, from setting up to packing up the drums. It is the drummer who maintains the rhythm in the band, and the best accent, or play around rhythms, dropping bombs, switching time, smacking out rim shots and making colour from cymbal splashes.

After rhythm comes deeper knowledge of the pulse and beat, or following the bass player. While the drummer creates the top end of beat, the bass player creates challenges around pulse. This is the beauty of practice, where good surfers can improvise even in the worst conditions. I practised and practised, paddling longer distances, surfing more often, riding slop even when others did not bother to go out, and sitting and watching the waves. Some days you are paddling against erratic, big, foam-headed phantoms playing howling, free jazz, drumming you down, so you must work hard to create rhythm from, and within, chop. The next, the wind goes around offshore, combing every unwinding face. The rhythm is self-evident with standard, walking bass line and a gentle drummer on brushes with plenty of work around the cymbals. You then surf the standards, with scintillating solos and a little bravado.

Right: A good day's work – with Zed Layson and Tristan Jenkin, Oman

4 No Brains, No Headaches

Perhaps the gods hang out their laundry on days like this, when everything seems torpid and slow-moving. The damp October sky hung like a wet cloth over a sullen sea. The mood was infectious. I paddled out, leaden, for my last surf before leaving West Penwith for Cambridge University. It was early, the world seemed empty, and suddenly also a lonely place. The water felt like crude oil – dense, resistant – and I felt sluggish. The slugs always come out in hordes on days like this, enticed by the 'mizzle' (half-way between mist and drizzle). In that head-space, it felt like the whole point of surfing was to do nothing, or at least to let things emerge from an uncluttered space. So I did nothing of consequence – just trimmed in a salute to the simple pleasure of gliding over water. The eerie stillness mixed with the piercing foghorn from the Longships lighthouse. I counted nine more slate-coloured waves, milked them to the dank sand, then walked up the hill at Gwenver, pausing for the slippery, ink-black slugs spread like commas across the cliffside that I could barely read, making me feel strangely nervous. The fact that I counted the waves made me think that perhaps these were my last for some time.

Surfing and the Cornish landscape had led me into studying geography – the human experience of place and space. Living on a massive Neolithic graveyard made out of the very bones of the earth – granite-lined tombs – but dedicating myself to the life-giving sport of surfing had induced a particular sense of place, and now that would be ruptured and I would be displaced. Maybe I was leaving both Cornwall and surfing behind on the long road to becoming an academic? More importantly, I was frightened that I might lose my wave-sense – that unique perception that comes from being close to the ocean – a weather-sensitive attitude. Was my sea-fitness going to be replaced by sensitivity to library, desk and computer? I thought, for all of its promise for my future learning as one of the top universities in the world, Cambridge might in some way blunt my outlook on life rather than sharpen it.

After that depressing dawn surf, I drove with my parents for seven hours to arrive at Pembroke, one of the more intimate Cambridge colleges. A crisp wind blew over manicured lawns and the air was dry. It felt refreshing in comparison with the steely Penwith coast. I was certainly the only person in the gathered undergraduates to have Atlantic salt patterning my eyelids. I wore the distinctive surfer's uniform, bringing an identity from which I could not escape. Even at those challenging interviews to gain a place at Cambridge many months earlier, under

Rolling thunder – Panaitan, Indones

pressure I called on instinct and timing from surfing. I did not hesitate, but arrived at simple, clear answers, hitting the mark like a cool blue note. Over a fourteenth-century worn stone floor, certainly trodden by some great people, my sea-sense emerged. The tutors were not testing applicants' scholarly knowledge, but their imagination. Einstein was right – imagination is more important than knowledge. Thank god for Dad's favourite surfing T-shirt with that slogan on it, and the infamous artwork by Californian Rick Rietveld, with Einstein playing a Hawaiian slack-key guitar! Sometimes pop culture prepares you for high culture. When the Cambridge-stamped envelope arrived in the post with news of the outcome of my interview, I spontaneously ran out to Escalls Cliff, overlooking Gwenver, as if I wanted to share the news, good or bad, with the sea-life, or maybe with those weather gods hanging out their washing. I nervously ripped open the letter – I was offered a place. The Einstein T-shirt became an icon in the family for a while, a reminder that imagination and intellect can meet.

Another great T-shirt that I borrowed from my dad was one that read simply: 'No brains, no headaches', in bright print across the back, accompanied by three cartoon pineapple faces with shades and sun-soaked smiles – 'No worries!' as the

he new geographers: with Italian Emi Cataldi – Oman

Australians say. It was a carefully constructed, tongue-in-cheek dig at the stereotype that surfers are fun-loving, happy-go-lucky opportunists with water on the brain – a beatnik tribe of anti-intellectuals. Beach bums in the 1950s, hippies and drop-outs in the 1960s, 'animals' in the 1970s shortboard era, aggro-punks in the 1980s, and always air-headed fashion victims, surfers have struggled to present an image that embraces intellect or academic interests.

Surfing and Cambridge did not immediately seem to mix. Yet there were role models – a number of champion surfers went on to become leading academics, mainly oceanographers, most famously Ricky Grigg in Hawaii. In the wake of their research on the conditions that produce waves, clearly the arena in which surfers could shine was the study of their liquid environment and its flux. Consider the massive number of variables that enable surfing – the meteorological and oceanographic phenomena that generate swell, the geographic location of the break, the geology of the reef or beach, not to mention the global industry that has supplied the wetsuit and chemicals-based surfboard.

Interwoven with the science are the cultural, humanities and artistic aspects of surfing, exploring style, the shaping of lifestyle and identity, and poetic questions about the 'feel' of a board or a wave, beyond the technical dimensions. Surfing has an expressive side, and this is just as open to study and debate. Binding it all is a collective folk wisdom from the surf culture framing a unique grasp of ocean dynamics. While surfers intuitively know about wave action and its relationship to bottom shape, these links are still unexplained fully by science. Beach studies fall within the realm of complexity theory. The beach and sea, as interacting living processes, operate not in a formal and predictable balanced position between order and chaos, but at maximum complexity on the edge of chaos, as a nonlinear, adaptive system. Surfing folklore is validated within the community of surfers, not in academic circles, so the surf culture produces lay geographers confident at predicting the outcome of a combination of topography, oceanography, meteorology and even 'crowd factor' on any given day. Organized, lay surfing knowledge is a great example of practice expertise in action, rather than 'specialist' knowing – a tacit knowledge developed through experience, but hard to articulate. The rewards for predicting the perfect wave at the perfect time are considered the perfect experience.

A short time into my degree and away from the sea, I realized how deeply my strength in character and fulfilment in life fully depended upon surfing regularly, immersed in that salt bath. Seven-hour drives to get my fix became a cyclic pattern, listening to Art Blakey hurtling around the high-hat and Hank Mobley quick-timing both sides of the beat. The lay-off periods produced a keen hunger, and I improvised against Cornwall's shifting drum and bass, the grind and pulse, the rhythm machine, with accented accompaniments, hooting until I was hoarse. After a typical weekend on coastal terrain, exchanging practised 'shakas' and 'high five' handshakes, I arrived early at an academic supervision with my personal tutor, a fine strand of seaweed still glued to my ear. He was the archetypal Oxbridge scholar – tweed jacket, his room stacked with early maps and leather-bound books. I casually held out my arm and unconsciously attempted a high five to thumb clasp. He was totally confused. So was I. A stiff-limbed response came from both of us. Then I switched back to the default mode – a firm and respectable handshake. I flushed crimson with embarrassment. It reminded me of my dad's story of a time when he went for a job interview. He had been surfing earlier that morning and changed in a hurry into his suit, forgetting, as always, that around the eyes would be telltale salt stains. Luckily, the interview was successful, but as Dad reached across the table to shake hands with the panel, he stooped enough for his sinuses to open and drain straight on to the table.

With international airports only a short drive from Cambridge, the anticipation of foreign shores helped me to focus on completing the round of essays necessary for tutorial sessions. Just hours after the last supervision of the first term

Overleaf: Dwarfed by the Tropics: with Welshman Elliot Dudley – the Philippine

I sped to Stansted and flew out to Arrecife, Lanzarote. I met friends working a charter on the 45-foot, steel-hulled yacht, *Norwegian Blue*. We sailed south to Los Lobos, straight into a bulky swell, easily predicted from the synoptic chart in the local Canarian newspaper. Lobos lit up for five days, with long wrapping rights, grinding over shallow, volcanic rock. On bright, low-tide mornings I shot the curl on high lines, soul arched, and rode the nose fooling gravity, like a saltwater scientist. I played with weight distribution, steering from the tip, applying and lifting pressure with my back foot. I went into swooping turns and accelerated, before sailing down the line again.

Through the inside section, where rocks would appear in the face of the wave, there was a lot of bottled energy that had not yet spun from the folding wall. As the curtain fell, it would always be at the point of splintering, so that the whole thing might collapse and drag you with it, sucked into the white water's manic conversation with itself. Here is where your coda counted, your final, drawn-out statement after the chorus, solo and second chorus. Sometimes there was an opportunity for a long, technically brilliant piece of bravado rather than a kick-out to safety. 'WIPEOUT!' sang the 1960s Californian guitar band, the Surfaris, before the drums kicked in, pummelled, and the guitar reverberated. My hubris showed. Pride before a fall. The coda was a step too far, and the wave worked me into its churning gut, trying to digest me whole. I charged along more monsters, but seeing danger ahead through the inside, learned to skim quickly out into the channel, smiling.

I was beginning to get the hang of surfing's 'total vision' – riding a wave is not a disconnected series of manoeuvres, but a combination of rhythm, timing and improvisation that embodies a whole round. Clear away all the talk about how excellent jazz musicians achieve such an intense level of improvisational skill, and you will be left with this holism – the note you are about to play is already preformed by the notes you have just played. The coming note occupies the space you have created for it, even at a tumbling pace. Listen to the late Johnny Griffin, once the fastest tenor on the planet, and it is all ease and grace, not force. Listen to a Sonny Rollins coda, walking the stage or the aisle, horn bobbing, in total concentration, and it seems to emerge as whole, an outpouring of joyous sound.

When the swell dropped, we motored north to Graciosa Island and made the most of its better exposure to the next Atlantic pulse. Eventually heading back south to Arrecife, a vicious south-east wind spat rain and desert sand all the way from the Sahara. The sea raged. Despite the conditions, I could not resist one last session. Everyone else was fatigued, but I jumped overboard to surf a spot locked to the cliff face in the north-east corner of Lanzarote. It was huge, forlorn and unhappy with itself, with great lumps of grumbling water knocking against neighbouring lumps. The yacht weaved its way out to sea between these thick, building lumps whipped by sudden gusts of wind. I could see the crew drop anchor far offshore because it was too rough to stay close to land.

Figuring out the line-up is always tricky when paddling in from behind. I had no idea what it was like until I funnelled into a wave. I took some screamers and did nothing but hold on tight and cannon for the safety of the shoulder. An hour or so later the tide had dropped, and the whole deep-water channel was closing out. If my friends had already tried to collect me in the zodiac, I had not noticed. I suspected they had, and pictured them back at the yacht brewing strong coffee over the swinging cooker, listening to a Tony Williams rhythm section, planning to come out again in another hour. The yacht looked like a toy boat on that vast, lumpy horizon. Waving was futile. I was not keen on surfing any longer in the out-of-control conditions, so I opted for the long, out-to-sea paddle.

I kept my head down. With spidery arms and angular elbows that I wheeled like oars, I was a quick paddler. At home, I had trained regularly along a gruelling cliff-edge route, then out to sea and back, with a run up the steep hill at Gwenver to end. I was half-way to the yacht, and sat on my board to check co-ordinates. Looking back, the cliffs had shrunk, but the yacht was still way out of reach. As I glanced north, I saw a big ship steaming out from the channel between Graciosa and Lanzarote. My antennae suddenly became alert – it seemed to be heading straight for me. It was *Submarine Vision*, an 80-foot, glass-bottomed boat that takes tourists on day trips – an exceptionally rough ride that day. Should I wait for it to pass, or try to paddle in front of it? As it got closer, I realized the best option was to wait. I did, until the huge vessel gouged past. I felt helpless seeing that thing mowing through the wide expanse of deep blue. Sightseers on deck were shocked. Some walked in awe to the back to get a better look. I had to duck-dive under the foaming wake of the boat. After that close call, the rest of the paddle back to the yacht seemed a breeze. I thought of the dozens of stories I had read about those early big-wave pioneers in Hawaii in danger of getting caught by horizon sets, and having to paddle miles to find the keyhole spot where they could venture in. And this was often in failing light.

Unpredictably, my surfing seemed to improve through weekday stints away from the coast in Cambridge. I stayed physically fit through football, yoga and a stretching routine, and mentally fit from reading, listening to lectures and writing. I studied a formal and informal curriculum: academic geography books, and videos of the surf stars – old Californian Malibu master Lance Carson, Australian shortboard revolution sensation Wayne Lynch, and Hawaiian-Californian David Nuuhiwa, who took 1960s noseriding to its zenith with a combination of speed and grace unmatched until Joel Tudor catwalked in the 1990s.

Fired up to make my mark, I started to compete as regularly as possible, and clinched the first of a number of national longboard titles. When the summer arrived, I booked a ferry ticket to Santander and set off for Europe, alone, to enter contests and explore the rich culture across the Channel. I managed the long, eye-watering drives by opening my senses to the sweet-smelling pine forests,

Inca gold on the doorstep – Mundaka, Basque coast

surfing my way through France. In Spain, I feasted on *tortilla* and *tapas*, living a basic existence off prize-money earnings. Portugal's caffeine coast was stimulating, keeping me focused for the drawn-out drive to The Netherlands, where I won a contest in a nut-brown North Sea. This started a cycle of numerous trips to Europe's Atlantic (and sometimes Mediterranean) coast every summer for the next ten years, mostly for contests.

That first international season culminated in winning the European Championships at summer's end in pitching, razor-sharp rights at Praia Grande, Portugal. Afterwards, the European sport clothing company, Oxbow, signed me up for a long-term surf sponsorship. I was officially a 'pro surfer' while still a student. Getting paid to surf? I had to pinch myself. But I quickly learned the intense commitment this entailed, and realized hard work was essential to keep this dream intact.

The focal point in life quickly became a balancing act between studying, competing, training and travelling. In Cambridge, I met a couple of fellow surfers reading for their degrees. We would check the weather charts before the weekend and head wherever it looked best – Cornwall, Devon, the South coast, the

North East, South Wales and even Norfolk. On a marginal swell, we called up a shop with a sea view in Cromer. 'It's flat with lumps,' said the shop assistant. That sounded like a description of clean waves, so we drove over and scored 3-foot rollers. The following morning, we were back at high-tide East Runton just after dawn. The wind had turned northerly, and it was messy, sour, and bitterly cold. There was a punchy, short right and left rearing up in the current-ridden mess. As we braved our part-frozen wetsuits, we soon realized that this peak was breaking off a sunken tractor! It was stuck in the sand, creating a potential rust-bucket for a reef. For one hour we snagged tight rides on this bizarre and hazardous set-up. Then the tide dropped out, revealing the whole tractor. We came in and three fishermen were walking down the beach, looking concerned. They told us that the tractor had been caught by the tide while pulling up a crab boat. They were waiting to salvage it as soon as the tide was low enough.

The 'tractor coast' served up more decent storm surfs, but foreign travel was my primary goal. After all, as a geographer I could justify this as 'fieldwork'. Geography literally means 'to write about the earth' and I saw this as a vocation, through surfing-related travel. Cambridge prized itself on a type of holism in geography – a grand overview, an embracing opinion. Growing up in Cornwall, it was the only subject that came close to making sense of my fascination with the intertwining of oceanography, geology and culture. The foundation of the course offered grounding in the history of science, the 'age of discovery' to geographers, and a period of European exploration when mariners, traders and settlers touched every continent except Antarctica. The interior 'blank spaces' of continents – terra incognita – were charted, and the world's coastlines were reproduced in map form.

In the lecture theatre, I had just been learning about Andean geomorphology and Spain's dramatic conquest throughout Ecuador in the sixteenth century. Spain's horse-riding, armour-wearing, cannon-firing conquistadors were believed to be godlike, and spread terror among the Indians. But when they finally battled their way to Quito, they found the city razed to the ground by the locals, who preferred destroying it to leaving it in the hands of the conquistadors. I could learn a lot from the supervisions and books, but I now had the chance to enter a new classroom of the real in South America, shooting for a surf film, travel documentary and a range of magazines.

In a typical juggle of contrasting commitments, I had just landed at Gatwick after a week-long assessed coursework trip to south-east Spain. I caught the bus to Cambridge. But I had to be back at Gatwick the following morning for the flight to Ecuador. My flat mates were all away as it was the Easter holidays. I frantically packed. In the fluster, I got in a hot sweat, stripped down to my boardshorts, opened the windows, then closed them because the draught was cold. I walked out of my room to the toilet. The door slammed behind me, and I heard the latch click shut! With no key, my only option was to climb in through the window, which I had just closed. I was in a mad rush to make the drive to the airport. I ran into the garden. It was freezing – clear, but piercing March air. I climbed up the drainpipe, hung on the windowsill, and wrenched open a small gap in the window where the wood had swelled from age and did not seal tightly. It broke and swung outwards at me. For a stretched-out, slow-ticking second, I soul arched backwards, hanging heels, cartwheeling my arms, and just avoided falling 2 metres. I dived through the window, over the table, and continued packing, then hauled the boards and bags out of the room. They clattered down the stairs and took out a few banisters. I had no time to deal with it, and raced to Gatwick. I had to beg the staff to let me check in so late and jump queues, and boarded by a hair's breadth. I slept practically the whole way to Ecuador, landing in Quito, 2,835 metres above sea level.

The next morning, a tempest rapped relentlessly against the hotel room window, daring me to go outside to explore. In synchrony with a clap of thunder, I got up awkwardly, in several stages, badly jet lagged. Outside, the gutters were overflowing on to the pavements. Everywhere I looked, I saw poverty. I did not feel uneasy, but strangely secure wandering around the damp *barrios*, where locals wore bowler hats, and the old grandmothers sat on doorsteps and behind rusted iron bars, their eyes and ears attuned through the years to the pulse of Quito, never missing a beat. On a pale blue balcony, shaken by earthquakes, standing proud, one *mujer* guided a needle and thread through a robe of white fabric – a wedding was imminent. Coupled with a scratchy Hispanic ballad leaking from the living-room radio, the picture quickly became a stereotype of traditional Latin America. Thankfully, the bubble was pierced by the shrieks of an actress in a *telenovelas* (soap opera) next door, yanking me back to the close of the twentieth century.

After lunch, our crew of professional surfers – including Welshman Chris Griffiths and Australian Beau Young – filmmakers and photographers met up. We began the treacherous descent down the Andes – single-laned, potholed, white-knuckle territory at the scary end of the travelometer. The Ecuadorian driver called it the backbone of his country – I took this in, literally, as my spine torqued. He turned around to look at us all in the back of his van every time he uttered a word, and in doing so, took his eyes off the steep, winding spine, threatening to career over the sheer drop, where we would fall hundreds of metres. The brakes squealed on corners like a crazed animal. We leaned out of the window and swore that we could see fluid leaking from the wheels. And then the brakes failed. The driver gripped the wheel tightly, guided the van around a fortuitously drawn-out corner and on to the straight, where he pulled up on the handbrake. We slowly came to a halt, just before the next bend. Beyond it was a small town, and we pushed the van in and found a mechanic, relieved to be alive.

Eventually, we made it to the lowlands – dusty roads, plantain fields, shrimp ponds and a blistering 40° Celsius. At sunset, we reached the ocean at Canoa. A huge north-west swell compressed lines across the whole coast. A pointbreak towards Colombia, reputedly one of South America's finest spots, would be exceptional. After a day acclimatizing, we drove into deepest northern Ecuador, where the recent El Niño rains had wiped out most of the bridges. Attempting to board a car ferry, we managed to get the wagon caught between the boat and the soft sand. While sinking, the engine failed, the exhaust drowned, and the whole vehicle filled with water. As we rescued it, and let it dry for an hour, the mosquito artillery was unbearable. A malaria epidemic had killed tens of thousands of locals, and we coated ourselves in pure Deet. Tragically, one of our local guides contracted brain malaria on this trip, and died months later. He did not take the anti-malarial tablets (or use the toxic repellent) that are a mainstay for many travellers.

Following a two-day drive, we had to abandon the van and loaded into pick-ups, continuing for hours along a stretch of beach littered with colourful conch shells. Then we climbed on to skips. Two hours later we cornered a headland and

Below: Quito's suburbs – Ecuador. Overleaf: Time out – Ecuador

caught a glimpse of a surreal, flawless, 300-metre-long lefthander. I laughed out loud at the cliché, as if Mother Nature was playing a joke on us – emerald green water, pelicans, never-ending empty rides, white-sand bay lined with palm-thatch beach huts and dense rain forest. Imagination may be more powerful than knowledge, but up to this point, such places were only in the imaginary, and I had no knowledge of their secrets. I thought to myself that this was too good to be true, and something had to go wrong.

Then one of the film crew stepped out of the skip with a camera on his shoulder. A wave pushed up the bow, and the skip smacked up from below, hitting his chin with force. It burst open like a soft fruit. Blood poured from the deep cut. As his jaw hung, so we hung momentarily in a bubble of inaction, slack-jawed with surprise and horror, and then snapped into action. It was eight hours to the nearest hospital, but he had to turn back with a couple of the Ecuadorians to make the trip as he was looking in bad shape. It was a sobering reminder of just how isolated we were, and how the unpredictable will always climb in through the cracks to haunt any off-the-beaten-track trip.

The waves at Mon Peche surpassed anything I had ever seen, or even dreamed of. Minute-long rides became the norm and two minutes the record. The take-off, at low tide, was shallow over lava reef, so you could lock-in for maximum speed, hang just under the hook; then run ahead of the pulse as the rhythm section wailed with exquisite tone. Chris was riding with incredible power and flow, slotting into the pitching tube and reinventing the cannon by blasting outlandish re-entries and cutbacks. Beau was giving ordinary moves a radical twist, and a stunning inversion. His on-rail speed, vertical grace, tube-riding, and bolt-upright hang tens were arguably the best in competitive world longboarding at that time – resulting in two world titles. From this trip I would switch to a long period of sponsorship on Chris's hand-shaped ultra lightweight boards, modelled on Beau's personal templates. They brought more power to my surfing, and I learned how to turn with a deeper arc. But at times, as the rookie of the crew, all I could do was just sit in the channel in awe, watching that double act improvising around bottom turns and cutbacks on those blistering walls.

A solid swell pumped and pumped, and our heartbeats kept pace as we got slotted, and sometimes cracked by the lip, imitating the way that we cracked crab claws for our food at surf's end, hungry but elated. Energized on more fresh fish, rice, bananas and fruit juice, we rode from dawn until dusk. I grasped the notion of holism (or dance) in surfing, and put it at the centre of my practice, feeling the pulse, hanging on to ringing notes for long noserides, and inscribing the faces through flowing turns. Pulse is the overall and additive rhythmic sense of a ride from takeoff to kick-out. If you do not feel the pulse of a wave as a surfer it will simply engulf you, leaving you in its wake. Listen to a great jazz bassist like Dave Holland and you feel this wonderful sense of 'push' underneath the other soloists, who ride on the back of the pulse he develops. Miles Davis used funk bass players brilliantly in the 1980s to create deep pulses that carried the music along and acted as a safety net. Oceans pulse naturally, thanks to the big weather drummers who smack at, and roll around, their skins, producing sets. The surfing sequence is a dance, life is a dance... the music is ready-made by the elements.

Travelling through Ecuador, and studying the 'age of discovery' back at university, stirred a longing for challenging travel. I wanted to walk in the footsteps of those great explorers, but, more importantly, to make my own footprints through surfing, in travelling with a conscience – carrying an ecological mindset. Ecuador gave me the chance to write numerous features to accompany the travel photography. And this exposure as a surfer and writer in a wide range of publications was lucrative advertising for Oxbow. They reciprocated by continuing my contract. Suddenly, Cambridge, surfing and travel gelled when economic reality kicked in. My professional career was sealed. When *Carve* magazine employed me as guest editor of an annual special issue, I saw that surf journalism would become a vital accompaniment to surfing itself.

There were many more trips, contests, magazine articles to write and edit, academic essays, dissertations and examinations. Most importantly, a Cambridge education is as much about forming character as accruing knowledge. The University loves rounded people. I was trying to mix two lifestyles, with geography, literally and metaphorically, as the glue. It worked, leading eventually to a Master of Arts degree. Days after my last exam I was defending my European Longboard title at Le Penon in Hossegor, France, and sitting an entirely different sort of examination. I got off to an awful start in the practical. I was flustered, anxious and surfing erratically – the gig was turning sour. My concentration seemed shot. While long lefts peeled down a shallow sandbar inviting a response through style, my timing was poor and I was hitting a series of bum notes and slurred scales. But the sea was suddenly stirred by a raking and intensifying wind, pushing the peak further out of reach. The gods were suddenly with me, and I found rhythm. The tiring paddle to the sweet spot began to work in my favour. All that hard paddle-training paid off. I began to out-paddle the field to pick off the best sets. I found space, elegance, oozing notes, searching phrases and took a second, consecutive, European title. Sweet soul music.

5 Taking the Tube to Work

After finishing university, I was able to devote myself wholeheartedly to professional surfing and travel writing. I got hooked on the antithesis to Cornish beachbreaks – tropical places, where billions of polyps grow and die to form razor-sharp, white coral reef beds – treadmills for big, cylindrical waves. I would picture myself locked into one of those barrels where time is frozen, then glide over the trap as the wave spat me out in its last gasp. At this point, I was clearly driven by the image that is so often portrayed in surf magazines and movies – the perfect wave. The archetype of the travelling surfer is the theme of the iconic 1960s Californian film *The Endless Summer* – lured by the promise of pristine peelers just around that next headland. This scenario is, of course, relative. The 'ultimate' ride is constantly evolving, ever-shifting. For some it is a no-limits tow into a big-wave monster, or a last-minute drop over a dredging, shallow reef. For others it is a clean, waist-high curl at sunrise, lingering and suspending time, with nobody else out. It is relative to your level of ability and experience in the first instance, but also relative to the opportunities you might generate for travel. Being sponsored to travel on photo-shoots is a rare blessing, even if it is earned.

The perfect ride is like the myth of the Eternal Return – all things must pass, only to be repeated – but concentrated into seconds of bliss. The shortest, but most concentrated, of journeys that is the tube ride is the prize at the crossroads, the intersection of two trips: the travelling surfer and the travelling wave, both long-haul veterans. But, while the wave travels free, and indeed gives us energy, the long-haul flight is a conundrum for eco-surfers. I found out in Ecuador that it is easy to exoticize and romanticize, especially when you go to places that are so different from your home. Pollution, poverty and illness are stark, often overpowering, realities for visitors from the 'first world' to the 'two-thirds world.' In Edward Said's *Orientalism*, he argues that the 'exotic' aspect of the Orient is basically a construction of the Occident – the western world's 'imaginary'. Surf magazines and films often do the same. They are almost pornographic in their depictions of surfing – glossy, sexy images of perfect waves, often tubes, and often shot from almost impossible angles – that most of us will never get to ride. We rarely see everyday footage, or even wipeouts – the sequences are carefully cut and edited. The fare begins to get hyper-real, and the line between reality and simulation is rubbed thin.

Right: Missed your train? Hollow Trees, the Mentawais, Indonesia

Even so, I was buzzing to follow in the footsteps of the great explorers and the modern-day surf travellers, to leave my own footprints and write about these experiences. Oddly enough, although I grew up in a household overflowing with books, I was never an avid reader. I read just enough to keep up my studies, but as a kid I was always more interested in doing something physical than in reading. I could have indulged myself early on in the postmodern novel, or the history of the Blue Note jazz label, but I did not catch up on reading until I saw that it was imperative if you are to be a writer. And travel writers, of course, must travel!

For me, travel starts in the mind's eye with a story already told to oneself, a journey of anticipation. My Indonesia rehearsal started as a teenager, when I drooled over magazine features – an endless mix of mind-boggling surf. I pined for Sumatra. Before I realized that dream on an organized magazine trip, my imagination had prepared the senses for a deeper experience through rehearsal. In sports, the arts and medicine, the better athletes, musicians and surgeons rehearse in imagination before the performance. Then the realities kick in.

Arriving in the Mentawais, I feel ready. In the soft light before sunrise, surreal rights peel across the reef at Hollow Trees. What was once virtual is unfolding before my eyes. On my first ride, I know I will get the barrel of my life. It will be unavoidable. I am just in trim, letting my fingers run through the wall. The lip folds over, and I am enveloped by a strange feeling of timelessness, and then rudely posted out. I take off deeper, and feel a cool zephyr blowing in my face. Light is filtered through an ever-thickening curtain. I am balanced, committed, playing hide-and-seek with the lip. I hold in tight, but in the back of my mind develop an image of a double-edged sword. This is a fatal mental error. All the best tropical waves are flung across a bed of nails – over sharp coral. I am on stage and per-forming, and this is the curtain razor. The transparent lip wavers and feathers at the shallowest section. The coin flips, the reef sucks dry, I am clipped in the midst of reverie and land flat on my backside getting dragged across the live coral heads over the 'surgeon's table'. Backstage, I am bleeding. The curtain has dropped and my performance is flunked. Surf travel opens you up in more ways than one. Travelling is also unravelling. Real memories are embedded in my skin. The wave is always your mistress – you must learn slowly through her instruction and not force the issue. The magazines and films do not show you this apprenticeship.

I surf the glitzy breaks in the Mentawais, from Macaronis to Rags Right to Bank Vaults. They are near mechanical, but the trip becomes so predictable that oddly, after a while, everything starts to look strangely humdrum. I am shocked at my attitude, because the adrenaline hit is fierce, and the hawk-like reef is waiting to claw me. The outer beauty of coral, a living structure, conceals the inner poison-ous beast, and it is only a matter of time before you pay your dues with an infected wound. Yellow hydrogen peroxide stains my legs from a few encounters already. If I have the confidence, ability, or maybe stupidity, I can push my surfing deeper and

Sundance at Sumba, East Nusa Tenggara

deeper until I find myself in parts of the wave so 'gnarly' – because only a surf adjective will get me there – that endorphins restructure my body and brain with a stamp of 'no fear'. Or, I wake up tasting the antiseptic in a Singapore hospital with my recently scissored skin painfully stitched. I walk the line between the two scenarios.

Surfing radical tubes for the first time, I often felt more like *Surfer* magazine's clumsy but loveable cartoon character Wilber Kookmeyer than Rick Griffin's radical Murphy – tucked back so far that the tube monster emerges from his lair and taps him on the shoulder. Death-defying tube riding was not my forte. Maybe this has something to do with wearing contact lenses. There is always a nagging feeling that they will be flipped out by a spit of spray as you eyeball the exit while the curtain falls in front of you, leaving you confused and lost at sea. In fact, on one particular wave I was so startled by the depth of the barrel that my eyes stayed wide open in amazement and both my contact lenses did wash out. In a nanosecond, my senses went from the most acute perception to half-blind blur. I had to paddle to the boat to get a replacement pair, by which time my rhythm was shot and I could not slot in again properly on that session.

Overleaf: Lush life – Bali

Locked on that boat, I felt strangely detached, as if I was doing what everybody else had done for years. In jazz, once the path-breakers such as the legends of bebop, die or move on, it makes life very difficult for the competent but uninventive imitators. Today, there are brilliant post-bop technical musicians who have graduated from jazz courses, and who have completely mastered the techniques of the trailblazers. But somehow, they can sound flat, uninspired. They can play runs at lightning speed and complex chord changes with ease, but this can sound like surface flash without a depth of feeling. There are many competent surfers who can ring the changes, but somehow you have seen it all before; something is missing, some brilliance of invention or quirkiness.

Today it is rare to meet a travelling surfer who has not experienced first-hand the sweet smell of *kreteks* (clove cigarettes) and the smiling faces of Indonesian children. Most recently the Mentawais has witnessed a surf travel onslaught as boat charters compete to access the waves, sometimes with little benefit to the islanders. The Indonesian invasion began in Bali back in 1970, when local taboos were challenged head-on as Hawaiian and Australian surfers Rusty Miller and Stephen Cooney paddled out at Uluwatu, filmed by Alby Falzon, owner and guiding spirit behind Australian *Tracks* surf magazine (actually a paper, based on the format of the American *Rolling Stone*). The Hindu Balinese considered swimming in the ocean a religious taboo. To locals, Uluwatu was 'the place of the living dead', populated with evil creatures and unsettled spirits. To enter the water was sacrilege. When the taboo was broken, simultaneously an unbroken tradition in a culture was snapped by an outside force – surfing. Unwittingly, this was a neo-imperialism. 'Conquering' Uluwatu was also walking all over a cultural tradition. Imagine being the first-generation Balinese surfers, where breaking the local taboo must have been far more risky than the presence of sea snakes and bone-crushing barrels. Falzon showcased Bali in his film *Morning of the Earth*, and Indonesia rapidly became an adventure outpost for surfers and the soil for a growing national surf community.

My first Indonesia experience was a package trip orientated around waves, waves and more waves. The flights were pre-booked, we were collected in Padang, and motored overnight offshore from Sumatra to the Mentawais on an 84-foot coast cutter at 12 knots, with ice-cold beers and hot, served food. I realized that I did not want to travel just because of the guarantee of the wave. That guarantee is the package holiday. For me, it lacks the unpredictable, the interaction with the locals on a non-commercial level, the cultural and geographical aspect of travel. When I got home, as a writer there was hardly a story to tell: predictable captions next to photographs selling the dream of another perfect wave in a mythical paradise. Discriminating readers grow tired of this. Pick up many surf magazines, and the writing can seem secondary to the photographs. I wanted the two to complement each other, to tell a story together.

Soul 'trane – Batu Islands, North Sumatra

I was anxious to find another angle, to go to unusual places where few people, if any, surfed. This was my quest for brilliant corners of the world. But I knew that I needed to combine the travel with unique photographic or film work to fulfil and maintain commitments to my sponsors Oxbow, who were providing a basic living wage. In the meantime, while I was amassing contacts and developing plans, I set out to improve my surfing ability, and to sharpen my travel senses in Costa Rica, Mexico, Barbados and Morocco. I also packed in intensive training at home and as many contests within Europe as I could enter. Soon this strategy paved the way to additional sponsorship from Vans. I was offered a berth on a promotional photoshoot to the remote Hinakos and Telos in North Sumatra, on the *Indies Explorer* – a 115-foot ketch, made from local ironwood like a traditional Sulawesi *pinisi* (two-masted ship). This, at last, had some unique flavour. I was back in Indonesia, through the back door of genuine exploration rather than the front door of surf tourism. John Callahan was hired as the photographer. I had prized the 1993 copy of *Surfer* magazine, with his stunning documentation of a pioneer trip to the Philippines, revealing the sizzling right-handers on Siargao. I had heard that he applied the highest standards to his art as a meticulous photographer, and I looked forward to getting to know him.

It is humid. It grips and presses on my chest, weighty, like a huge tarball, wringing out sweat with the slightest exertion. We wait in a low-budget, seedy, hotel bar in Padang called the Depo – otherwise known as the 'Deep Hole', for its tendency to 'bury' misguided travellers in days and nights of delirium. Deranged karaoke whines, permanently it seems, and becomes part of the furniture. We play pool on the sloping table, soon to drive to the harbour to board the boat. On the front door to the bar, a white sign reads 'no ecstasy', with the 'c' and 'y' peeled off due to the relentless action of the humidity. The door swings open, as in a spaghetti western. There is, however, no 'man with no name'. John appears, sweating, just like the rest of us. He wears a white peaked cap, a plain, all-white, long sleeved T-shirt, and sneakers. I like his understated style. He looks like a young John Malkovich playing the role of an eccentric surf photographer in a Hollywood movie about a sweaty bar in Indonesia. I do a double take.

The boat has character – sails that whip and lash, rigging that sings at night as the wind races through it – and with a long fuel range we are days at sea, soon out of sight of other surfboats. John is an avid reader, well educated, articulate, a thinker. I can tell from his photographic work that he can bring a touch of beauty to the otherwise mundane. He has a keen sensibility, and banal conversation will definitely not be tolerated. This is no 'hey dude!' surf trip. We strike up a conversation about music.

Surfing and music have always been closely linked, and travellers are now blessed with readily portable catalogues. Californian friend Maia Norman – surfer, designer, mother, and partner of the artist Damien Hirst – had just introduced me to the iPod in Costa Rica. Given that music and surfing feed each other, and that the surf movie is the place where the two can meet, such soundtracks are often disappointing – predictable and bland. An activity that thrives on challenge has spawned a culture that does not seem to be attracted to challenging music, and shuns certain genres. If jazz is chosen for a surf film it is predictably cocktail jazz, easy-listening, jazz lite – never a serious bite of Charles Mingus or David Murray, or a deliberately slightly off-key Ornette Coleman, whose depth, tone and melodic invention match the aesthetic of engaged wave-riding. Surfing and classical music is not a pairing that readily comes to mind, yet the minimalist movement in longboarding (back to basics, retro, no leash) so easily resonates with the work of John Adams or Steve Reich. Listen to the opening track of *The Night of the Cookers*, a live Blue Note album from 1965, where the trumpeters Freddie Hubbard and Lee Morgan trade off licks at their peak, at breakneck intensity. This catches perfectly the slightly hysterical feeling of flying down the line with the curtain about to fall that I was now fully tasting in Indonesia.

When we started surfing, John's work ethic was strict and masterful. He had developed a kind of all-terrain, all-weather, bionic 'shooting' outfit. It meant dealing readily with boat, zodiac and land. He could forage through foliage, get waist-deep in water, and emerge from a swamp, unfazed. He could handle mosquitoes (they never seem to bite him), heat, sun, nagging children, while calmly smoking a cigarette and talking to the local fishermen to get insider knowledge of the coast. He always got the shots, with total devotion to his art, a master at work. If the light was good, and the surfers were not ready, he had a store of signs, stares, gestures and comments that made you get your act together instantly – 'You surf, I shoot.' His attitude is that you get out what you put in. Importantly, if the surf was not good, we would still 'go to work'. There was always potential material, a story to source, landscapes and communities to interact with. John provided a motivation for me to surf hard, but also, he educated an eye for the context of the trip – his commitment to capturing cultural lifestyle, through place, artefact, or people, is supreme. John taught me that the surfing trip is just one lens through which to view cultures. The footprints we see on the sand of the 'unsurfed' beach are not those of the intruder, but those of the local inhabitant. We have not 'discovered' any surf break. We are guests, often uninvited, of those who already live here.

The waves in the Telos did not peel like those polished faces in the Mentawais. They were tighter, sharper, harder to ride. The reefs had knots, the faces bent, lips twisted. In the Hinakos, at the steamrolling lefts of Asu, I had some nerve-racking moments, followed by some of the best rides of my life. Against frantic tubes I unzipped down the line, the wave biting at me, just held up enough for me to slot in and play a waling note held at intense pitch, suddenly snipped short in a last ditch kick-out, the curtain coming down like a guillotine, the audience already set for the next act. Bawa, close by, was a shifting, deep-water right with a long drop, big sections and an inside bowl. On a huge wave outback one of the crew was bottom turning into a ludicrous tube. Then the lip clattered him so hard on the head that he was sent into a cartwheel, ripping his T-shirt to shreds. I was watching in horror. During the lull I paddled to the impact zone, but he did not surface for seconds. A whirlpool marked his rise, and slowly his arms emerged. It is always a bad sign when the head is not first to break the surface, sucking in air. His face finally welled up, his eyes yolky. He was groaning, clearly in excruciating pain, his ripped shirt hanging off his shoulders. I pulled him on to my board with the help of another surfer – his ear was bleeding and exuding white gunge. The captain of the Indies Explorer called a doctor in Singapore on the satellite phone for advice, and stitched up his wounds. He had burst his eardrum, and had to sit out and watch for the remainder of the trip, numbed on Bintang beers and strong painkillers.

Between big swells during one unforgettable session in the Batu Islands the surf appeared to billow, like a sari in the breeze. The light slanted and the faces were as smooth as silk as they rippled and unfurled. I surfed alone and weaved around a long, waist-high wall. At one point I swayed one way casually on the nose in a gentle soul arch, while the palms behind swayed, as they do permanently, the

Chasin' the 'trane – Batu Islands, North Sumatra

other way. John captured it perfectly on camera. It is a moment of improvisation, going against the grain, balancing opposites, playing around the beat. It remains my favourite shot, beautifully composed and framed. Later, John joined me on my spare board. A thin band of haze created a spectacular aurora effect from sunset to moonrise. We traded a few more waves before dark. Our friendship was sealed.

The boat journey fulfilled the necessities for the advertising campaign. But these commercial ventures, where the client paid a small fee for the use of a large amount of photographic material, lacked creativity. This kind of thing was becoming so widespread that in the magazines the adverts and copy were becoming indistinguishable, as if the surf culture was beginning to parody itself. John had been a staff photographer for mainstream magazines, but now preferred specializing in adventurous freelance trips where he could sell as many interesting pictures as possible for widespread editorial. He supported the more cultured, alternative publications that did justice to his imagery (and the articles that went with them). He was a master at email networking – clear and considerate – and perfected a breakneck turnaround to deliver the material for printing. He preferred to work with an eclectic mix of international riders – not necessarily top-drawer pro surfers, but adept, often bi-lingual travellers and interesting characters. He also liked to use locals from the regions he was exploring. Crucially for me, John had built up a wide array of contacts that would open doors for my writing.

As guest editor of an annual magazine special before the dominance of digital, I had the privilege of trawling through a wide variety of images from many of the great contemporary surfing photographers. When I spread a selection of John's lifestyle and surfing slides across the lightbox and looked at them through the 'loop', I quietly punched the air. He had an incredible talent for capturing the moment in images that portrayed more than just action, but an essence. Back home, I studied material from some of John's early explorations that featured in various magazines I had collected – Angola, India and Myanmar. I craved to write about what John loved to capture through his lens – the idiosyncratic moment, the curves and inflections in the natural environment that flip you into a new understanding, surfing in settings where you can let the culture stain you with its difference, and offer paradoxes. I looked at the atlas one evening – all 195 countries – and circled every stretch of coast that had to have rideable waves. Swathes of Africa, Asia, the Caribbean and South America all had surf that had never been reported in the rapidly growing international surfing media, and would offer fascinating geography. To fill this list would take generations of devoted travel. I wanted to make a start. So when John emailed me to join him on a trip to the Maluku Islands in north-east Indonesia as surfer and writer, I jumped at the chance.

Manado, in North Sulawesi, is an ugly, fast-developing urban mess, smothered by carbon monoxide fumes. It somehow exudes greed, and I am glad to pass quickly through this sprawl to meet a mix of South African and European shortboarders (who would become close friends over the years) in a small harbour, just outside the city. This is the downside of surf travel – having to land in, and move through, ubiquitous Americanized cityscapes that are simulacra of other Americanized cityscapes. *Murex*, the boat we have chartered, is moored up. It is normally destined for calm waters due north of Manado, where divers explore war wrecks. The Indonesian boat crew load our equipment and supplies while John and I talk to the American captain. He tells us he has never been to the Malukus. It is, allegedly, way too dangerous with heavy clashes between Christians and Muslims. But the UN adviser to the region gave us the green light to travel there. We ask if he is coming. He says the less English-speaking confusion on board the better, and advises us to just let the Indonesians deal with everything and always stay on the boat. British friend Eugene Tollemarche is well versed in the Indonesian way, having spent long periods living feral on various islands and working as a chef on surf charter boats. He is now fluent in Indonesian, and will be essential to this trip. Eugene, John and I have maps, and unroll the sea charts on board with the Indonesian captain, co-ordinating our route by pinpointing places that might have good waves, with promising coastal configuration, bathymetry, bottom shapes and reef formations. We have a swell forecast, a tide chart, and a pencilled agenda.

Eugene Tollemarch measuring the lip

After a gruelling 60 hours at sea, heading east from Manado, the north Malukus come into view. Ancient, pristine rainforest is unbroken, save for ribbons of cascading water. We ask the captain to move closer to land, because the map reveals a choice set-up for a long left-hander. I make out a dot of a village – Sopi. Copra smoke fills the air. Clouds from the burning coconut husks shroud a ruby-coloured mosque. A sweaty wave throws off fine threads of foam from its back as it peels in the direction of the mosque, finally expiring in a dark green rivermouth. John is poised with his camera equipment. We all dive off the boat. As we paddle over to the reef, villagers line the shore. They cheer as the shortboarders take off on the first set, and launch into their routines with flashes of exposed rail, working at the edges, riding the lip and pulling its energy ragged. I dance with a wave all the way through to the inside lagoon, the ovation onshore becoming louder and louder, until the water turns buttery, so that my feet slip and the whole crowd laughs as one as I tangle in my own steps.

To my amazement, seven local kids paddle out on wooden bellyboards. At the inside bowl, three of them swing back into the surge and skim to shore, hooting. I paddle over, and invite one of the boys to ride my longboard – an aerospace-inspired composite, light years ahead of his crude equipment – but he shyly refuses. The next set peaks, reels, fades, and then reforms on the inside bowl. We both catch it in a cascade of notes, runs and arpeggios. There may be more than 5,000 languages still spoken around the world, but just six emotions are shown universally through the face – happiness, sadness, anger, fear, disgust and surprise. We only need the first and last to communicate the essence of surfing and sharing. We speak the common language of respect for the sea and total immersion in the senses, and ride that wave all the way to shore.

The light is poor for surf photography, so the village becomes a more appealing proposition. John steps off the zodiac on to the beach. Eugene paddles in, and we are greeted with enthusiasm. At first, the place smells rancid. Copra tinges everything, but that scent of burning, fermenting coconut husks dripping with oil gets sweeter, until I actually start to like it. The youngsters are lost for words. They have never seen a Caucasian face. Once part of the spice trail, harvesting nutmeg, mace and cloves in the sixteenth and seventeenth centuries, the Maluku Islands became so remote that in 1973 a Japanese soldier was found hiding in the mountains after 28 years, convinced the Second World War was still happening. He had to be lured from the jungle with a loudspeaker playing an archaic Japanese anthem. He handed back his gun, which was still working, and his last five bullets.

An old man with wispy hair tours us through the village and invites us to sit down in a stone-floored room. It echoes the noises of the jungle, the shiver of the trees. A table is full of ashtrays dusted with the remains of *kreteks*. John passes the man a cigarette. They light up. Eugene confirms that we are the first visiting westerners in over a decade. There are no signs of the religious turbulence the American captain warned us about here, but, rather, a traditional lifestyle, unsullied and at peace.

Back on the beach some of the locals have come in, dripping wet. I pick up one of the kids' bellyboards. Curved-nose, square tail, 3-foot – it is the same shape as Sandwich Islands depictions from Captain Cook's voyages. In the late eighteenth century, Cook and his crew, aboard the *Resolution* and *Discovery*, became the first Europeans to make recorded contact with the Hawaiian Islands, and witnessed surfing off Kauai, while the ship's artist sketched an exaggerated picture of near-naked natives sliding on carved wood planks. Cook made landfall at Waimea harbour in Kauai, and sycophantically named Hawaii the 'Sandwich Islands' after the Chief of the British Navy, the Earl of Sandwich. It was a typical imperialist conceit, as if the Hawaiians did not have their own names and history. They did – and their history was filled with surfing. In this remote corner of eastern Indonesia, the locals had independently evolved a wave-riding culture, mirroring that of the Polynesians. At Waikiki or East of Sulawesi, the ocean seems to dictate a basic sense of how to design a surfboard.

John was raised in Honolulu, Hawaii, inspired by a sport that the post-Cook missionaries nearly wiped out. While British contact and imported disease almost killed all the natives, Protestant-Calvinist missionaries repressed surfing due to its nudity and perceived frivolity. Work, not play, was the stern philosophy, and surfing was 'against the laws of God'. Ultimately, surfing would be revived in Hawaii as tourism and beach culture became popular in the early 1900s among the affluent. It became a symbol for American tourists, a mark of a healthy lifestyle. The Hawaiian double Olympic swimming gold medallist, Duke Kahanamoku, was recognized internationally as the emissary of surfing. Modern jazz and modern surfing are thus grounded in two Dukes – Duke Ellington and Duke Kahanamoku – two great improvisers who made things look and sound easy. Both were masters of the lazy sound – music rolling like water, watersports played like music. Jazz surfers must want to be like these Dukes, making the difficult look easy, stuff just rolling out as if it were second nature, where actually it is carefully constructed, painstakingly learned, beautifully improvised, but now honed. And right here in Sopi we watch the last local ride effortlessly ashore on his wooden board, his cool notes disappearing slowly into the big bell of the sky.

'Growing up on a tiny chain of islands scattered in the vast immensity of the North Pacific Ocean, it was an inspiration to see what the rest of the world was like,' said John. He went to university in California, and soon embarked on extensive travelling. Eventually he based himself in Singapore, as an ideal place to develop his *tropicalpix* photography business, specializing in exploratory surf trips. The opposite to the war photographer in magazine copy, John nevertheless shares the same love for the impact zone. Anything could happen at Sopi, but we meet with a warm and generous people who share our love of surfing.

We refuel and restock in Tobelo – a sharp contrast to the sparsely populated Sopi. It is a small port, but seems to be brought to a boil by the heat, and more than buzzes in near bedlam. I sit by a roadside stall as motorbikes speed past with men on a mission. I am a detached spectator from the land of nervous energy and high levels of psychological stress. Here, the stress is physical. One man on a motorbike carries a crate of spiky green fruits, pulls over and drops it at the stall. The fruit reeks – it is durian, the king of tropical fruits. While it smells like a drain and has a cheese-like texture, when you break one open, it tastes like a mix of tropical juices in one, with a top note of cream. The fleecy clouds thicken to the consistency of milkshake, suddenly darken, and gather as thunderheads. The water drumrolls against the tin roofs, like Art Blakey leading his band from behind, stalking the horn players, with pulse and beat raining down the soloists.

Close to Tobelo, we sail north through an impressive concentration of reef passes. But there is only a small swell, so we keep exploring the north of Halmahera, and inspect the whole coast of Morotai. On land, Muslim villages sit beside Christian villages without strife, as expected, but in apparent peace. The coast is blanketed by rainforest. We wade into a dense tangle, meeting a spectrum of greens, from viridian to light pea. The vegetation is teeming with malarial mosquitoes and there is surely some lurking, unfriendly wildlife. From atop a waterfall, the smouldering volcanoes in the distance look like time bombs ready to explode. Even the sky seems to hold that omnipresent threat of eruption, and the ground feels ready to split. Maybe these perceptions are also, classically, those of the visitor not the local. I feel more comfortable as I see that near these volcanoes the small waves close-out in front of steep cliffs that fall into the Pacific basin in a very slow swoon.

Eventually the sea stirs from its torpor, swell rises, and we find a first-class wave in the most unlikely of places. A left peak swerves with a soft shoulder, until it bends through the shallow inside bowl into a slingshot of a barrel, over a live reef. I watch the cranes fishing on the reef, offering a model of patience, as I wait for a set. A crane dips through the giant lens and spears the fish, compensating for refraction. I read the wave's refraction as it bends towards me on the critical take-off. The glare of the sun from the water compounds the issue, and my eyes become increasingly bloodshot. The water is so clear that I cannot see the curvature of the face, but seeping diesel from the boat ironically marks the shapes with a slick, and for a moment there is both function and beauty in pollution. The seduction is short-lived, as the fuel forms a film on my board and I slip on the next ride. We linger for the remainder of the swell, syncopating solos, working the angles to perfection, and head home after weeks at sea.

On subsequent boat trips, we surveyed more corners of Indonesia's expansive coast, using maps and charts to check reef passes, promising-looking headlands, bays and coves. Although Bali has embraced surfing wholeheartedly, and is bursting at the seams with numbers, a lifetime exploring the 34,000 miles of coastline spread around 17,000 islands (11,000 of which are uninhabited) would merely scratch the surface of the wave potential. Even Indonesia's Indian Ocean understudy, the Maldives, has a staggering choice of unridden options, where turquoise waves bend around atolls and break like sheet glass, scattering water shards.

As we continued to explore, I meticulously noted every detail in my journal and on copied maps. I loved the way we moved from myth to map, like the European story of exploration, representing a concern to convert cosmological theory into cartographical reality. We soon started to use Google Earth satellite imagery printouts – a hyper-real way of spotting perfect waves. But getting to these spots in the real, rather than the virtual, is a different challenge, a question of separating satellite image from reality. I thrived on the idea that we had an incentive beyond the personal experience, publishing photos and stories, and planting seeds to motivate others to maybe follow in our footsteps, or make their own footprints. Importantly, the international magazine *The Surfer's Path* had become a firm supporter of our projects, embracing the creative copy and ensuring an outlet for more alternative trips. Back home, friends and acquaintances talked to me about this 'dream job', unaware of the wider issues – preparing for a trip with rigorous research, but no guidebooks or magazine features to reference; keeping in shape; getting the right medical advice; fulfilling contracts from surf companies; balancing the financial costs I had to pay myself with the possible rewards in writing commissions or continued sponsorship, not to mention the risks of the trip itself. These were not holidays, but intensive, yet immensely rewarding, work experiences.

6 Manila Dawn

Manila's dawns are dark and smog-ridden, with steaming mountains of trash punctuating the insistent vocabulary of the shantytowns. I nearly gag on the stench. Rats must be everywhere, a cholera or typhoid epidemic in the making. Garbage has a special political relevance in the Philippines. In the latter years of the Marcos presidency, a burning dump nicknamed 'smoky mountain' became a symbol of the leader's disregard for the poor. Eventually, an avalanche of filth killed hundreds of people. The chaos remains, now a permanent feature. But among the squalor is also a lustre – the collective body of polished chrome on colourful jeepney buses begins to reflect the sunrise, and it dances among the moving bodies. Every decorated surface gathers and redoubles the light – religious icons, horns, aerials and mirrors. Each bus has its own nameplate, and is stuffed to bursting point with passengers. Like mobile artworks, they pump smoke, scaling up and down the keyboard that is their particular and familiar route, to pick up and drop off more passengers. Brakes slam with audible force like the drummer coming down with both sticks at the end of a solo, heavy on the snare's rim. Driving here is like drumming in a freeform band – you have to anticipate every elastic snap back and sudden change of rhythm. There are no speed limits, or, rather, no limits to speed except speed itself. No warnings pop up to slow you down or take a detour. Manila is jazz in a bottle, but the decision to drink is all yours.

Sashaying through the jeepneys, tricycles with tiny, roofed sidecars bolted to a 125cc motorbike, scratch and rap, wood against metal, metal against flesh. They spit out toxic fumes from their crude two-stroke engines. As I choke on the smoke, I notice a fast-food restaurant, appropriately named ChowKing. Crowds are thick and flocking. The sun pulls sweat stains from their backs that never seem to bump, but leave sweet smelling trails over ragged roads. Grey cement becomes urban coral, shot through by sunlight. Life washes around hot metal, machines and monuments. Even a wedge of sidewalk, below a highway and between the angles of a junction, is filled with a bed and a family who quietly comb for scraps among the chaos. This is their daily living.

The truth drug of Manila street life brings you bolt upright, until it bursts open like a case of a ripe fruit. You have to bring your sleep into alignment with the

Right: Ostentatious, moi? – Palawan
Overleaf: It don't mean a thing if it ain't got that swing – Nagpan

place, so that you wake at the heart of the turbulence. This is just the same as a three-wave hold-down on a big day, a severe wipeout. You cannot afford to fight it. You have to go with the turbulence. The writer Joseph Conrad said that at birth one falls into a dream, like falling into the sea. So, in a sense, life is a big hold-down. Some fight it. Some roll with it. Travel brings you right up against these paradoxes. For years, I idealized Milius' *Big Wednesday*, and then I heard about the reality of what he put the actors and surfers through. Peter Townend, who played the surfing double of Jack, the good guy of the trio of heroes (the only one who goes to Vietnam), recalls filming the surf scenes in El Salvador during a civil war (because it was too crowded in California), where travel needed a serious military escort and he suffered from a bad case of amoebic dysentery. For all the wrong reasons, this turned out to be his most memorable surf trip.

For me, the Philippines does not induce a dark heart of the body, like Townend's bout of 'Montezuma's revenge', but a state of mind. Once you get away from Manila, the epicentre, you sense great beauty. Meandering up the west coast of Luzon, past garlic and onion groves, tobacco fields and rice paddies, allows the mind to unwind, the body to surface from the turbulence, and gulp a little clear air. Up here, the Iberian code of *mañana* – 'Filipino time' – has clearly outlived America's attempt to impose a protestant work ethic. There is a legacy of double imperialism: the US in the first half of the twentieth century and, preceding them for 400 years, the Spanish. The collision of colonists is plain to see. Skeletons of Catholic churches resting in lush greenery collide with a star-spangled McDonald's parade, complete with Ronald the Hamburglar, mounds of fries and lashings of cola – a postmodern fiesta.

We arrive at La Union, home to the country's original surf scene, thanks to its proximity to the old US military bases. A local Filipino national champion and surf coach is teaching the president's daughter to surf. The government have put snipers on the beach, while two navy ships patrol the shore – anyone catching a wave other than the president's daughter will be shot! The current president is so popular that in some places her name replaces 'female' on bathroom doors. But these things can change quickly – turbulent zones equal volatile politics. Recall the Marcos era, with Imelda's extensive and clearly fetishistic collection of shoes (a symptom of political psychosis).

The locals tell us that Car-rile point is breaking. It is a rivermouth, sculpting the waves into kilometre-long rights. The outflowing sediment produces dark water, but with the blistering dry-season sunshine, the waves are a reverse of the legendary Costa Rican points of Boca Barranca and Pavones, but with fewer surfers. The water-fist unclenches on take-off to swat me. I am hauled over at the heels. The wipeout is a reminder to get my traction – feet-on-wax-on-board-on-water, toes relaxed, uncurled, arch of the foot dropped, dead weight, look down the line, flow into the turn, walk to the nose, toes over – traction regained – the cross-

Putting your shirt on it, and a big winner
– Luzon, the Philippines

step and the three-step rule: invoke, enjoy, repeat. The breaking curl presses down the tail, dragging the fins for phenomenally long noserides. On one wave, the gush of the face gathers underneath and cushions the nose for a personal record-breaking 40-second hang five. On the inside, as the tide drops, the flat reef is alive with spongy seaweed, making it safe to keep on that cascading coil until the fins just cannot find enough water to cut through, and I kick out, wriggling with electricity.

On Sunday, I watch the twin rituals of cockfight and gambling in Ilocos Norte. Washed in special shampoos and raised on specific diets, two well-groomed birds are shown off to the gathering crowd. There is plenty of money at stake. More than people can afford. But these rituals are lifeblood. The cocks look harmless until three-inch blades are attached to their ankles. They peck each other before the fight, but are held back. This seems to stir up their aggression. The gamblers analyse the spectacle, and the stakes change. The blades are sterilized with alcohol.

The ring of spectators tightens, moves closer in common anticipation, and the cocks are set free to fight. There is an audible swish of feathers, a hiss of blades, and they are quickly deep in combat, striking and drawing blood, kicking up dust. But the real fight is in the audience, who are pulled back and forth by the urge to gamble more, and begin to identify with the tussling birds. The sound is deafening and agonizing: brute energies and animal sacrifice. The two fighting birds are halved in a final winner-takes-all strike of the blade, while some lucky punters double their money. The unlucky are spurred on by an intricate web of signs and omens to recoup their bets at the next fight. Ritual and addiction stand hand-in-hand at the ringside. Dust and feathers settle. The champion is whisked away, maybe to a waiting surgeon to attend to his injuries. The loser may end up as the evening stew, or, for the great fighters, is immortalized and buried with honours in a nearby graveyard. Successful bets are quickly turned into drink, where celebration and commiseration mingle equally and set together, as the sun falls, into a common collapsed body at day's end. All such male-bonding activity ends in exhaustion.

We head back to Manila. As the first photographer to document surfing in the Philippines, followed by a string of pioneering trips, John has become quite a celebrity here. He introduces me to some expatriate Japanese friends, opening surf shops and schools to capitalize on the Filipino surf boom. They try to entice us to invest time and energy in their businesses, claiming that in Japan they are surf bums, but in the Philippines, everybody wants to do business with them. We politely decline the offer, and fly to Palawan to explore a portion of uncharted surf that stretches from the Mindoro Strait down to the tip of Borneo. Our boards do not fit on the Domier 228 nineteen-seater aircraft that connects to El Nido, where the best waves are likely to be, in the north-west reaches of Palawan, so we touch down to the south, in the carefree regional capital, Puerto Princessa, unexpectedly greeted by a party for the 10th Annual Austronesian Linguistics Conference. A marching brass band is in full swing, and the academics who filled the plane are welcomed with coral-bead necklaces. They mistake us for delegates. Thoughts about the good and bad faces of globalization cross my mind, but I do not piece together a coherent thesis, and prefer to linger with the creative confusion, in the spirit of the country we are visiting. I think of the strange and rather beautiful collision of cultures that occurs at the expense of jet-travel pollution.

'Are you here for the conference?' 'Of course,' I reply, getting a necklace placed over my head and playing into the serendipity of events, thinking of our surf exploration team as anthropologists of a kind. 'I'm studying the Tagbunura

Approach with caution – typhoon swell, east coast, the Philippines

tribe's ancient dialect, and how it encapsulates their deeply animist beliefs,' I say, regurgitating something I had learned at Cambridge about an isolated group in northern Palawan. A little dissimulation spices up the occasion. I feel guilty, however, as I think about the academic furore caused when it was discovered that an 'unknown' tribe trapped in a Stone Age lifestyle in the rugged heartland of Mindanao's South Cotabato Province, the Tasaday, turned out to be a hoax supported by the Philippines government. The Tasaday were supposedly located by helicopter in 1971, and photographs were released of people wearing crude loincloths and using stone tools. The *National Geographic* ran an extensive feature entitled 'First Glimpse of a Stone Age Tribe', exposing the 27 cave-dwellers who apparently foraged to survive. Even the famous mythographer Joseph Campbell was taken in, and included an account of the Tasaday in his masterwork on world religions and myths. The academic community had been fooled wholesale – it turned out that the Tasaday were Manabo people being used as pawns in a complex government-backed, land-grabbing ruse. Promised cash and protection, they posed as primitives while their land was sold off to timber contractors.

I change the subject to avoid embarrassment, explaining that our group are primarily in Palawan on a photographic project. Faced with a gruelling twelve-hour drive north, we hurriedly overload a hired Toyota Hyace, and meet our driver, Goyro, who lives where we are heading – El Nido. At speed, we bounce all over the unpaved roadway, and finally burst a tyre. This literal exhaustion, I figure,

Rock music for small people – El Nido
Left: Not 'verti-go!' – El Nido

is all part of the master plan – the Philippines seems to be based on a pneumatic principle of pumped-up chiefs and a deflated populace – desperately trying to understand how a corrupt economy has not long since burst wide open and deflated.

Wrestling with these paradoxes, suddenly it all makes sense when I am told about the mythology that runs through the culture. Goryo explains that the faster you go in the Philippines, the longer it takes. This slightly perplexing moral comes from the fable of an old man travelling with a horse heavily laden with fresh coconuts. He asked a boy if it would be best to move quickly or go slowly in order to reach his home before nightfall. The boy said he would get home sooner if he travelled slowly. Refusing to believe this, the man hurried his horse along, but the coconuts kept falling off, so he rushed faster to make up lost time, but again and again he had to reload the coconuts. Eventually he got home, but long after nightfall.

Despite the bustle of Manila, Filipinos generally resist the psychologically manic tempo typical of the West. Goryo keeps saying it's 'just a while', or 'just over there'. He has no sense of time or distance. This might explain the sporadic timing of the morning church bell I had noticed throughout the trip so far. *Bahala na* – 'happens what may' – indicates blind faith in the will of God, so Filipinos do not plan for the future as fervently as they live in the present. They accept that fate will take its course, for better or for worse. 'Fix it when it's broken' is Goryo's solution. So when we top up with oil, fill up with gas, and spend hours sourcing a spare tyre, I realize that he has not prepared his van in any sense for the trip.

Late the following morning, we finally arrive in the north, ringed in alabaster sand, dark rings around our eyes. The sea is flat calm, so after a long rest we subscribe to the modestly advertised 'walk to El Nido's 250-million-year-old limestone summits'. There is no guide, but sandal-wearing Goryo knows the route. Only in the Philippines would such novice climbers be led with no harnesses or helmets, just the awkward fit of finger and toe to crevice and ledge, up a near-vertical limestone mountain. This is the closest I have come to my life hanging by a thread. In a strong moment of relief at reaching safety at the top of the summit, Goryo says, 'When Filipinos climb Everest, they'll be the first to do it in flip-flops.' I stare down from the summit at El Nido nesting in a startling bay of lagoons and vaulting cliffs. Goryo points to constellations of dark stars on the limestone cliff faces. They are swiflet nests, literally glued to the rock. Birds' nest soup has been valued highly as a culinary delicacy and for its health properties for generations, bringing Chinese merchants to El Nido – 'The Nest' – since the early thirteenth century. The locals gracefully scale these majestic faces for the sticky nests. Imagine farming vertically, instead of horizontally, to handpick your crop!

Back at sea level, the Iberian attitude of *mañana* is dominant. The ocean seems to have caught this spirit, as the swell on this visit is too slack to refract around the surrounding reefbreaks. Nagpan, a traditional fishing village 30 miles north of El Nido, is better exposed to the surf, which starts to build. The place is packed with bamboo-woven walls, palm-thatched roofs, and front gardens ablaze with bougainvillea. A north swell brings new waves, groomed by the rivermouth sand deposits. I think about grooming the music, deliberately slowing down through a cutback to stay in the pocket and follow the wave's curves, as the face pitches a little, allows for a rebound, and then cushions for a stall, four cross steps, toes over the nose, and a lilting hang five, Filipino-style: as indirect as possible. This way, you enter the solo at maximum intensity, but then shape it with variety and

punctuation, following the lead of a master such as Stan Getz, who could play at double time but still make the music sound languid, elastic. Long rides deposit you on the silty shoreline, the sound of the waves reverberating around the towering limestone cliffs like tribal drummers, the peeling rivermouth wave a repeating, breathy bamboo flute, waiting for something or somebody to finger the stops.

What is brilliant about surfers such as Joel Tudor today and David Nuuiwha from the 1960s is how cool and loose they look on a wave. This is because of that element of style that is creating space. When Miles Davis started to leave spaces in his playing – long pauses, with less emphasis upon flashy runs – every note counted, and tone became as important as speed. In Davis' 'less is more' sound of 'cool' jazz, understatement with precise timing beat flashy overstatement. Cool jazz played badly is just lazy, but Davis had brilliant tone. Thelonius Monk was also a master of leaving space, to just hang in the air. Sometimes, his pauses feel awkward, but they are there to provoke rather than soothe. Joel Tudor never over-eggs the pudding, or does too many, unnecessary manoeuvres on a wave. Every turn seems functional yet elegant. Riding the nose is perfectly weighted. Moves are stitched together seamlessly, with long pauses. Compare that with the slash-and-tear style of other surfers who have reincarnated as Charlie Parker or Sonny Stitt, the kings of speed, putting in as many notes as possible. Surfers who create space do not stall unnecessarily – in fact, some can be sultans of speed, but their speed is a long arc of silence drawn gracefully, leaving hardly a trace, merely a whisper, on the wave. Laird Hamilton is master of this on impossible walls of water that would send others into a jittery skate across the face, or break a person in two. He gets this cool from his step-dad, Billy Hamilton, the longboard master of understatement.

En route home from Manila I stay with John in Singapore. Bustling Boon Tong Kee is the city at its best. Clock towers, colonnades and technocrats mingle with hard-driving Asian capitalism, and are left to simmer together. When a tropical downpour suddenly lets loose, it sizzles off the road and there is a cacophony of scents – rain on hot cement mixed with soft fruit, fresh fish just turning, turmeric and cumin, and pungent meat grilling in the open air. Enhanced by the damp, the smells in Asia seem urgent, up close, and mirror the complexity-on-a-plate that is Asian cuisine. We eat delicately flavoured chicken-rice, and talk about new projects. The discussion turns to Africa, which arguably offers more adventure, colour, and empty coastline than any other continent. John has undertaken a number of extreme Africa trips, often with legendary American surf traveller Randy Rarick. 'There is war and poverty there,' says John, 'but also talent, ingenuity, and an irrepressible *joie de vivre* that is unstoppable in overcoming the obstacles and setbacks of everyday life in extremely difficult circumstances.' Africa beckons, and a pocket of anticipation develops deep in my gut like a rumbling drumroll.

Left: Vertical farming for swiflet nests – El Nido

7 Staying Tuned in Kenya

I feel a strange presence in the murky Kenyan line-up. I lie on my board, looking towards the deep channel, and meet the eye of a tiger shark. Her penetrating stare scorches my nerves. Red sulphur rushes through me and turns black and cold inside. Adrenaline pumps and gathers as a sour taste, like ash coating my tongue. Dread and hot surprise collide, as existence is suddenly shrunk to a pinhead. The formula is straightforward: predator and prey. In the stark clarity of the aftershock, I realize that if we had not exchanged gazes, I would already be in the throes of an attack. The shark would not have shown herself unless she was simply curious. I recognize, deep in my bones, her position at the apex of the food triangle. I also recognize the visit of a familiar. Poised with indecision, I keep staring at the black mirror of her pupil. Absolute fear gives way to gradual flight and the incoming rush of relief, although my nerves are fried and my gut has turned to tar or 4 metres of unravelled torque. Four metres of carnivore slips inch by inch below the surface of the brown, muddy water. She was languishing, nerves at rest, rather than wired for attack. She moves gracefully away with the current, my heart pounding, but also leaving me with a peculiar sense of calm.

When you travel in Africa, you need a broad mind, fully grounded in your senses. Do not challenge nature, but adapt. Stick with your animal instincts and keep cool – otherwise your first wave at some new break may be your last. Then relax into the place as invited guest, not the new owner. This applies particularly to the animal world. In shamanism, familiarity does not breed contempt, but respect. The familiar showed herself to be a host, albeit one with a reputation. South African friend Cheyne Cottrell (whom I met on the Malukus boat trip) and I stick together like glue, walking back up the left pointbreak at Ras Kitau between rides, deliberating on each occasion if it is worth paddling back out. But we do. Trust the host's ingrained ways and slip into the household with due respect. No flashy turns, just safe surfing. The shark appears again, but far away in the channel with the ebbing tide, drifting sinuously. She seems to know what we are doing. We know that she is the boss. We walk back to our beach *bandas* on Manda Island with John and gather our senses. The skies open. There is the rising animal smell of rain pitting dusty earth. Our Kenyan safari has begun with a warning: stay tuned, keep your eyes and ears open, respect the ancients. Be as an animal. Relax your gut.

After the shark encounter, we abandon our boards and walk for hours around the rugged, convoluted, rocky rim of the island with Kenya-based, Cornish friend Rachael Feiler. We are surrounded by a gnarled, impenetrable mass of mangrove

Red mist descending – Shela beac

roots that look like giant spiders standing high on the inlet banks. The air is humid, the tide low, the water still. We are stuck in stinking mud. Confused by the Swahili clock – which starts at 6 a.m. rather than 12 midnight – we have mistimed high tide. At Takwa, in south Manda, where the estuary encroaches the island, life is ruled by the tides. The rendezvous with the dhow is impossible since it is now low water. We force ourselves through a stagnant soup of deepening, squelching silt. We think the estuary opens out adequately to accommodate the dhow, but it cannot get close enough to pick us out of this swamp, and we wait, sink further and wonder what to do. Fiddler crabs scurry into their mud homes, and I think of the venomous green mambas that may lurk close by. I extract myself from the unctuous mud and climb up the tangled branches of a salty mangrove. The dhow is in sight, clearly unable to make it over the shallow bank. 'Do you think there are any crocodiles in here?' I shout to the crew as I volunteer to swim out to the boat. But it is sharks that are on my mind.

Splashing manically, I practically doggy-paddle with dread to the dhow. I stop, stand, and realize it has only been thigh-deep the whole way! 'No *papas* (sharks) in here – too shallow,' assures Answali, the dhow captain. I signal to the others to walk out. John hoists his camera gear above his head and makes it to the dhow without a splash on his kit. We all climb aboard the boat, but it instantly runs aground, so we wade 90 metres through silty water up to our thighs, taking over

the symbolic work of the engraved dhow eyes that have led these weathered vessels through the Arab world for centuries. I look into that dhow eye and see shark eye. I push and heave. *'Haraka, haraka haina baraka'* – 'Hurry, hurry has no blessing,' says Answali. Unwind that gut, breathe, play slower.

Sailing into the deeper channel, Answali tells me there are plenty of tiger sharks out beyond the reef. The rain and murky waters must have brought the shark in, because it is rare to see them in such shallow waters. Perhaps the shark was interested in an even rarer sight – that of surfers. In fact, we are the first surfers the locals have encountered. But these islands are used to other species of visitors. For ten centuries most of the settlements on the Lamu archipelago have flourished as small trading stations blending East African Bantu roots with Arab influence. The Arab traders would arrive in their dhows with the north-east trade winds (known locally as the *kaskazi*), and return on the south-easterly *kuzi* trades – a pattern reflected throughout the Zanzibar archipelago to the south in Tanzania, famed, like the Malukus, for its historic spice production. As Lamu blossomed, a distinct African-Arab Swahili culture emerged, shaped by the local wind, tide and terrain, detached from the Kenyan mainland. This is a place where culture has learned from nature.

We live in a world of snapshots. Tourists come and go. People visit these islands, fall for the mesmerising enclave of traditional Swahili architecture, the lack of cars, and the unfussy barefoot atmosphere, but fear the place will soon be ruined – over-developed, over-priced, and over-visited. Actually, Manda and Lamu have always been hosting new names and 'developing'. The Swahili style is to welcome the new, in order to sophisticate the culture. The Swahili are not a tribe, but a mixing – of Bantu, Arab, Persian, Indian, European and East Asian. The future is in safe hands here. Swahili culture is organic and dynamic, accommodating and adaptive. It seems to siphon off the most useful and graceful elements of knowledge and lifestyle from incomers, without compromising its heritage, adding layers to what is there that enrich. This is a truly syncretic place. While humans come and go, what persists is an underlying bigger beat – the natural cycle of the trade winds, the slow growth of baobab trees bearing up under these relentless winds, the pulse of the tide, and the audible heave of the mangrove swamps.

We sail to north-west Manda, where the scheduled plane wavers, lands and rattles to a halt in a swathe cleared in the thick mangrove. I remember the blast of sultry heat that engulfed me when I arrived. Then I am slack-jawed to see a longboard being unloaded. It is Randy Rarick's. Mine was sent on a more circuitous route – by larger plane to Mombassa, another to Malindi, and then by bus and boat to Lamu. Only Hawaii's Sunset Beach resident Randy has the knack of squeezing 9-foot plus into the six-foot-deep hold of a thirty-five-seater SAAB 370.

Left: Tuning the rig – Lamu channel, Kenya

The team is complete as Italian friends Emi Cataldi and Nik Zanella (whom I also met on the Malukus boat trip) arrive – from Rome and Ravenna respectively. Having already spent a few days in the area, I know our mix of international surfers will be welcomed as another bright stitch in the social tapestry that makes these islands unique.

It is late, and we head to Peponi Bar on Lamu for Kenya-brewed Tusker beers. For Randy, this is yet another addition to a long list of African adventures. 'Hi, I'm Randy.' 'I'm not,' replied the not-so-horny Cape Town girl on Rarick's first trip to Africa in 1971. Today, Randy is famous in surfing circles, as a board-shaper, a director of high-profile surf contests, including the pinnacle of competitive shortboarding, The Triple Crown on Hawaii's North Shore, and an organizer of the world's largest vintage board auctions. But throughout his career, Randy has amassed extensive Africa travel: nearly 30 trips to South Africa, plus Mauritania, Senegal, Ghana, Angola, São Tomé, Namibia, Mozambique, Malawi, Madagascar, the Comoros, Liberia, and Egypt. In fact, when he was hired as location scout for Bruce Brown's film *The Endless Summer II*, he scanned the whole coast of West Africa in a seaplane, marking every potential break on detailed maps.

Over another ice-cold Tusker, Randy entertains most of Peponi Bar with his story of the arrival from Namibia in a Land Rover at the Angolan border, half an hour before it closed at 6 p.m, in 1973. The guards were too lazy to do the paperwork, so they told him to come back in the morning. He pitched his tent right there, next to customs. But up the road in Angola was a cantina that started buzzing with music and activity after dark. He could not resist, so he climbed over the low fence and walked up the road to the cantina, where Portuguese soldiers were drinking and dancing. Two of them turned out to be the same guards from the border hut, but in this context they were delighted to see a new face and stacked up the spirits. By 2 a.m. the cantina closed, the word-slurring soldiers staggered out, demanding that they take Randy in their jeep with a spotlight to shoot leopard and deer. Next morning, the guards he had been drinking with stamped his passport – officially, soberly. Not a word was exchanged. Randy proceeded to explore the whole 950-mile Angolan coast, broke a half-shaft in the desert, nearly got trampled by a herd of elephants, and came home with malaria, but said that all the perfectly foiled, unfolding point breaks he surfed made it worthwhile.

Waking up in a towering 500-year-old baobab treehouse, I spot a cluster of bright birds flitting from branch to branch. Rachael and her mum, Helen Feiler (a Cornish jeweller), have built a room around their beloved baobab at Diamond Beach ecotourism resort on a prime patch of land in Manda. The tree bursts through the palm-thatched roof and walls, tangling with the large veranda. I watch a display of turquoise and red carmen bee-eaters and kingfishers courting

Right: On the waterfront – Lamu

and dancing on the *bandas* towards the sea. The onshore wind is so strong that there is clearly no rush to taste the surf. At breakfast, eating mango, papaya, and banana drizzled with lime, I ask Rachael how long the baobab lives. She tells me that in African folklore the baobab does not die, but simply disappears, like magic. Lasting thousands of years, the baobab is able to endure seemingly endless periods without water, and is near impossible to kill. Burned or stripped, she still grows. When she does die, she simply rots from the inside and suddenly collapses, leaving a heap of fibres.

In one of those serendipitous moments, just before this conversation I had been listening to Orchestra Baobab, a hugely popular band from Senegal in West Africa, who fuse Cuban and African music and have gone through several incarnations since the 1970s. I was enjoying their melodic, delicate dance tunes on *Specialist in all Styles*. It was produced by Nick Gold (who made the legendary *Buena Vista Social Club* album in Cuba, reviving the careers of a number of musicians) and Senegalese singer Youssou N'Dour. Again, coincidentally, I had recently met Nick at a party near my home overlooking Gwenver. His family has a holiday home in St Ives. I talked to him about West African music. This convergence confirms the global village – a tapestry of creative activity, Cornwall bridging to Africa through jewellery, music, surfing and ecotourism. But it is far from plain sailing creating an eco-lodge where amenities are scarce. The soft-spoken Swahili electrician explains to Rachael that there is a problem: 'The problem is we need to solve the problem, then the problem will be fixed,' he continues, scratching his head, clearly perplexed by the problem, which he fixes three hours later, closing the open electrical circuit. His patience is enviable. 'Little by little fills the jug,' goes the Swahili saying, mirroring similar sayings from the world's brilliant corners that go against the western way of impatience, short attention span and immediate gratification, bolstered by the collapse of time into the instant of the Internet.

Answali arrives wearing a rumpled linen shirt and green *kikoy* skirt. A kilo of the strongest *kolombo miraa* pokes out from his pouch. He chews the red-green bark shrub with bubble gum, and we set sail in the dhow across the deep estuary from Manda to Shela beach. Water laps against the hull that is stained with shark-liver oil, while the triangular *lateen* sail billows, then stretches taut in the south-east wind. On this crossing, no point of a fin breaks the surface. *Miraa* (an amphetamine-like stimulant) apparently makes your sight sharper, but Answali still manages to beach the dhow when he drops us off. '*Hakuna matata*' – 'No worries,' he says, calmly. We spend the next 30 minutes lifting and hoisting the weighty boat back into the Indian Ocean.

In the high era of bebop and postbop in the 1940s and 1950s, great jazz players were infamous for taking heroin. The word went around that heroin slowed

Left: A tree for the night? Baobab and tree house, Diamond Beach, Manda

everything down in your mind, so that you could play at the speed of Charlie Parker with your fingers, as your mind saw each note appearing separately. Being high on heroin was also called being 'strung out'. Stringing the notes together was then easier, it was said. It was a disastrous rumour as many young lives were wasted living this myth. Players who weaned themselves off heroin like Sonny Rollins, John Coltrane and Miles Davis said that their playing deteriorated when they were wasted. Seeing the notes in a rapid sequence of triplets suspended in time was a mental trick you could learn without dope, and this is the experience that is reproduced in that eerie, but ecstatic, moment when time stands still in the tube, on the nose, or as you pop up from a duck-dive and inhabit the rainbow-spectrum glasshouse on the other side of the wave made by offshore wind spray.

Shela is a 7-mile swathe of sand on Lamu that the locals consider crowded if more than ten people can be seen there. One of the new glitterati residents is Madame Peugeot (of the car dynasty). She walks past with her poodles and two Masaai warriors. Answali chuckles, and explains that since an eagle swooped to attack her dogs, she has employed warriors to guard them. Strikingly tall and slender, dressed in red cloth tied over one shoulder, the two Masaai have huge feet and thick ankles. Nomads, evolved to walk long distances. Armed with spear, sword, club, and braided hair, these warriors developed a fearsome reputation during the Western 'scramble for Africa' in the nineteenth century. They called the Europeans, who came swaddled in excess clothing, *yoridaa enjekat* – 'those who confine their farts'. The tourist industry on Lamu offers the Masaai a new outlet for their cultural pride, evident in their fine beadwork and basketry. But being paid to guard poodles surely has to be a first.

A few Kenyans flock to fill sandbags for cement, loading them on to the backs of donkeys. They will mix this with coral rag from a mine in Manda. With perfect timing, one of them touts a basket of fresh samosas, which we all devour. I pay him a few notes, and he tells me that life here is like an acacia tree, because you need little to survive. One tourist allegedly supports 30 local jobs. Answali asks the samosa vendor if he has found any *ambari* today, but he shakes his head. This waxy matter is the last remnant of whale excrement; to an *ambari* dealer is worth thousands of pounds. We walk to the exposed west end of Shela, keeping our eyes peeled for this priceless *ambari*. The wind is unyielding. But it is also our saviour as its fetch creates consistent, if imperfect, surf. The faces are dusted in spray, and the peaks are surprisingly powerful, but we are just as conscious of the unseen, predatory sea-life. Cheyne and Emi take Answali's twelve-year-old cousin for his first surf. He cannot swim, but stays in waist-deep water. He revels in the experience, does not give up, and keeps singing 'Just one more wave, just one more wave, just one more wave,' as he masters a clean ride, turning a Swahili chant into surf music.

I wake up early on Friday to the sound of a muezzin from Lamu, echoing in the distance and deepening in tone on its journey. I wonder how surfing would

Above: Island hopping – Lamu channel
Right: Learning to solo – Shela beach

sit with an Imam teaching in the local school. Would it be treated as frivolous and without sacred significance? We sail into Lamu, and wander around a tangle of streets. Swahili women, draped in their black *bui-bui* veils, glide through the shaded alleys, silent and inscrutable, only to vanish around a corner into an ornately carved wooden doorway. Barefoot, I find myself outside Jumaa ('sword-sharpening place') mosque kicking a football with the local kids. The rest of the crew join in. Then comes the third call of the day to Allah: 'Hello, God is great. God is great,' but we carry on playing. The muezzin on the PA gets louder

Swahili cats and Swahili slats

and louder and louder, until it erupts: 'STOP PLAYING FOOTBALL!' I cut my toe at that moment on a blade-like stone. The wound flares up into a tropical infection that requires a course of antibiotics on my return home. Karma is not just a Hindu notion, but clearly inhabits Islam. The 23 mosques in Lamu contribute to a much-respected Islamic teaching area. For faithful participants, Maulidi, a week-long celebration of Mohammed's birth, is so laden with *baraka* (blessings) that some say two trips to Lamu are worth one to Mecca in the eyes of God.

Back on Manda I wash the sand from my cut toe in the open clay pot, filled with flower petals, at the foot of the baobab treehouse. We eat grilled king fish, coconut rice and spinach. Unlike Lamu, a place of sounds, Manda is silent. The only beat is the music of the tide and the wind in the mangrove. The sky is the noisiest element, so studded with busy stars that it seems to shout. The racket of a tractor engine approaches at dawn. A red Massey Ferguson 165 with trailer pulls up outside the driftwood entrance to Diamond Beach, complete with foam mattress and pillows. In return for our help in floating his beached dhow at Shela, Answali has agreed to drive us in the only wagon on Manda to help continue our detailed mapping of waves in the area. We load into the trailer and an image of the 'tractor coast' in Norfolk pops into my head. No two places could be so different.

We pass giant baobabs and acacias, the coral rag quarry, Answali's maize farm, pairs of tiny dik-dik antelope, and walk through the ruined village of Takwa. The doors all face north-east towards Mecca, but the colourful mosaic cistern for washing outside the central mosque has not been used since the seventeenth century. Takwa was abandoned because the wells had become salty. Her inhabitants crossed the channel to Lamu Island, and established the town of Shela.

A short walk beyond Takwa there is a rocky right-hand pointbreak, bending enough into the wind to peel crisply over the shallow coral blisters. We wait for the tide to rise and paddle out. This is Manda's Malibu with a rough edge. I enjoy the loose California connection, stroll to the tip, settle, hover, and hang. One of those surfing moments that indelibly marks the memory. Randy elegantly navigates the nasal passage, and shows poise through subtle rail-work and ringing turns. Surfing with Randy offers a wonderful insight to surfing's past, present and future. He learned in the 1960s when Bruce Brown films, such as *Barefoot Adventure*, had a cool West coast jazz soundtrack. He was at the heart of professional shortboarding in the 1970s, and spearheaded the original world tour, then wholeheartedly embraced surfing's rebirth of longboard cool in the 1980s and '90s. Throughout the last ten years he has stayed right on the pulse, working innovative angles, and weaving them through surfing's industry and culture.

Randy's surfing style is beautifully eclectic and totally functional – excelling on all boards and all waves. He has great rhythm, and can switch rhythms as he responds to the moods of the unfolding wave. Sometimes he seems to be surfing with several rhythms at once, tuning in to that motion and multiplying its moods so that his moves arise fluidly out of the cross-rhythms of the wave. The longboarder's cross-stepping is a carefully orchestrated way of weighting and unweighting the board to create good trim, but it is rarely even. Walking the board is a polyrhythm, a shift, a nudge, a bold step, a pause, a retreat, all put together so quickly that the outward appearance is co-ordination. Actually, the movement of the feet offers a weaving of many points of balance. Elvin Jones was the master of polyrhythm – playing rhythms across left and right hands, and between feet and fingers. Tony Williams brought this to fruition, sounding the drums as if a solo instrument, not accompanying sax and trumpet but playing with an equal presence.

The following day we take the tractor as far to the east as possible, through the dunes, where turtles nest, to find a heavy beachbreak with a baking offshore wind. The crew charge into the powerful shorebreak – in response to the aerials Cheyne launches from crème-coloured lips, the gathered crowd of local goat

Randy Rarick shows the way

farmers and miners perform acrobatic back flips on the beach. Human footprints pit the sand to add to last night's loggerhead turtle tracks. After months at sea, across distances that take us hours to fly, the turtles come home to nest here, where they were born. Their co-ordinates are the angle of the sun and the unique and recognizable smell of the coastline. If there is a model for the benefits of travel, it is the loggerhead, unchanged for millennia, a template for survival of species through early adaptation. There is a powerful lesson to be learned from all sea life, so well adapted. Humans work against currents and winds, powering machines, to journey in the straightest possible line. But this is hugely inefficient. Turtles use the currents to travel. Dolphins in pods leap so high because they work collaboratively to produce strong vortices and eddies in the water that supplement their muscle power, allowing them to burst higher and further than their standing body mass should allow.

Night falls. The sea absorbs and cancels the light, turning ink black. The following morning, the sun appears to rise suddenly, gathering itself from the sea and drying out, gently shaking off the night sweats as an abnormally calm wind.

There is an atmosphere of anticipation. Ras Kitau point is looking classy. By now, we are familiar faces to the few locals we encounter walking to the point. The endless Swahili greetings that are central to Kenyan sociability – 'Mambo, Jambo, Hujambo, Sijambo, Habari' are offered liberally. Habari – literally 'news' – can be combined with anything to form a variation of 'How are you today, how did you sleep, how did you wake up, and how are you since yesterday?' But one of the local fishermen confesses that he is waiting for us to be eaten alive by the tiger shark. That would be news!

At high tide, the wave runs down the flat reef, the current slackens, and the rides are good. I can feel the tiger shark's presence, and humbly acknowledge her position as the local in this line-up, at the top of the pecking order. In the god's own country, always honour the god. One set wave peels off for 100 metres, and I get at the wave's energy, and exploit this through torque and tight turns, setting the pace for surprisingly long hang tens like a horn solo on circular breathing. I must be running off the adrenaline from that eerie encounter with the black-eyed One.

By evening, the swell has died and we do catch the shark's shadow before seeing her fin cut through the surface. I am secretly pleased for her continued presence, as she is now a familiar. Randy climbs the ruins of a sixteenth-century Portuguese fort to take pictures, and with a dhow silhouetted against the amber sunset the scene is unforgettable. Suddenly, the whole corner of the old fort gives way, and Randy falls about 2 metres into broken coral and ancient bits of canon, but emerges unscathed. Surfing 15-foot Sunset is a far more challenging drop. Randy tells me about waiting patiently for a ferocious, fast-moving west peak to feather, then clawing in, taking the drop, and lining up for a huge tube through the inside bowl. Most pinch shut, but some stay wide open and let you out into the channel as your insides erupt. Relax the gut, we are in Kenya. Breathe easy.

Surf adventures are full of heroic accounts of conquering and claiming. In Kenya we conquered nothing, claimed nothing. But the trip felt complete. We made countless walks to look around the next headland, just in case. That perfect wave was not around the corner. That pristine peeler was not over the sand dune. But circumnavigating an island, and exploring an archipelago, is a total adventure. We had done a lot of walking, like the Masaai who have roamed this chunk of Africa for centuries; and a lot of sailing, like the dhows that ply these waters. We never found any *ambari*; we did not discover a new surfing Mecca; but I learned much from sensing the rhythm and spirit of this remote African island: an intertidal, wind-kissed world, part rooted in mangrove and silica sand, and blessed with a Swahili culture, cool-headed in the heat of change. I like to think we left having given some joy, just as the locals gave us such hospitality, leaving only footprints, and not the bad after-taste left by ungracious tourists.

Overleaf: Send it by airmail – Cheyne Cottrell, Manc

8 Panamania

It seems obvious that if you travel with longboards, you have to plan ahead. But sometimes you just assume that things will work out. I arrive at Panama City's Albrook domestic airport for the short flight to Bocas del Toro on the Caribbean coast, near the Costa Rican border. With the prospect of a small aeroplane and a long board, I try to employ some of the tricks I learned from Randy in Kenya. Despite my best efforts, the baggage attendant insists '*La tabla no queda*' – 'The board does not fit.' I sweet-talk my way on to the runway and personally attempt to squeeze it into the hold from every angle. But the small twenty-seater can only accommodate 6-foot boards. The captain assures me that tomorrow the plane will be nearly empty, so they can place the board in the aisle. I have my doubts, and contemplate staying in the capital and taking the eighteen-hour bus ride to the coast with my board in hand. But I am persuaded to take the flight, convinced that I can collect the board at the coastal airport the following day. I take off, deflated. Travelling with longboards can be challenging: small baggage holds, top-heavy board charges. But for me the rewards are worthwhile – an instrument that works in all conditions and can be shared with anyone.

Quick-moving swell unloads out of deep water on to a rapidly shelving beach. This is a shockingly heavy break, far more powerful than I expect. I body-surf the 6-foot shore-dump and get so pounded that my head is ringing like a bell. My sinuses fill. They are already painfully infected from over-exposure to the cold Cornish winter back home. I feel like a blocked drain that someone has just filled in flushing away a bag of needles. The sharp pains spread as my legs are ravaged in the evening by *chitras* (sand flies), and at night they bleed from constant scratching. The next day, I ride a borrowed, battered, beastly longboard with a three-inch, sawn-down single fin. It is the only spare in Bocas, but in the powerful waves, and with little stability in the fin, it is like wrestling an alligator. Improvisation disintegrates into noise. I hang on to some outrageous drops, tottering on the back corner of the tail, then literally yanking the outside rail with my hand to pull the beast up into trim, and aim for the shoulder, which winds in to a gritty closeout, forcing me to get pitched, nailed and pulled across the sand in a cruel rubdown. This jazz does not swing – I listen in my mind, but not with my body and soul.

The duty manager at Aeroplas Regional in Panama City says on the telephone that the board is coming tonight. The plane had apparently been full every day, so they could not send it in the aisle space. But it does not arrive for days. Things get worse. The best reef spits out stern tubes cranking left in front of a huge smoul-

Borrowed time – Bocas del Toro, Panama

dering garbage dump. One hour into the session, inhaling fumes from burning plastic, I start to feel light-headed. Paddling in through shallow water over the sharp, urchin-infested coral offers another headache. My feet are cut to shreds, I cannot get a wink of sleep, and when I do, I have nightmares about losing my surfboard for ever, riding the stiff 'alligator' for three weeks, and being anni-hilated by hordes of *chitras* that tear the skin off my legs. Welcome to Panama – historical conflict zone. Welcome to Pana-mania – the local condition of per-sistent irritability.

I hear that the Panamanians sleep facing the mountains, so they do not have nightmares. I try this out, but my nightmares simply transfer to daylight. Half-way through the trip and I am still foaming at the mouth with no board, trying to survive intense, wedging waves on the cumbersome 'alligator', my normally fine-tuned gag reflexes muted due to the sinus infection. Finally, I persuade the airport staff to give up on the idea of putting the board in the aeroplane's aisle, but instead, to send it by bus. Panama City to the coast is a day and night ride on the route that will take my board, so I am not about to fly back and accompany it myself.

The longboarder's burden

The following morning, I take a water taxi to the mainland to check on my board's arrival. The rain is incessant, the drops drilling through my clothes. In what was once a bustling market town, wrecked by banana disease and an earthquake, I sit and wait in possibly the most uninspiring, fly-ridden bus terminal in Central America. The Creole receptionist tells me that the bus is three hours late. Apparently, at the last stop inland they found two unclaimed suitcases in the baggage – one contained $55,000, the other was full of cocaine. It turns out the whole bus was meticulously searched, every passenger and every suitcase. My unaccompanied longboard evidently caused a bit of a stir. It was the only other unclaimed piece of luggage – no name, no owner, but thankfully not stuffed with cocaine.

Through the downpour, the coughing and spluttering bus finally limps into the depot. My face lights up at the sight of my white board bag. When I unzip it, the board is intact. I thank the bus driver profusely, catch the next ferry back to the island and carefully choreograph the delicate hop over the urchin bed at one of the breaks. I paddle straight into a heavy set and snap my board clean in two – win some, lose some!

From Panama I head to Barbados to catch up with Bajan legend and good friend Zed Layson. His company reignites my surfing flame, and as we toast in indigo-blue breaks licked by wind and barbequed seafood, I clear my sinuses and heal bodily wear and tear, surf new waves and ride new boards. Jazz surfers must reinvent style on a regular basis, trying equipment and learning to play with challenging bands, gaining a new repertoire. All good jazz musicians are fluid improvisers, but little can match tenor saxophonist Sonny Rollins live, striding up and down the stage playing a half-hour solo, with tumbling notes, strident, high-register honks, developing into a fluid calypso and then a parody of a calypso powered by circular breathing so that there seem to be no gaps, no apparent in-breath, just dancing notes. But at the top of his career in 1959, Sonny Rollins felt that he had got stuck in a groove and wanted to reinvent his playing. He took a three-year sabbatical from public performance and recording, and made regular trips to the Williamsburg Bridge in New York, where he would practise eight hours a day, re-thinking his style. The result was a stunning album – *The Bridge* – showing a better-developed tone and an ear for more radical improvisation. Playing solos, improvising against the pulse of the elements, requires a good ear to hear that pulse. Knowledge of the bass line of the sea is the building block of good surfing, as it develops discrimination between which waves you choose in a set, where you sit on take-off, and which sets you leave alone – often close-outs.

I fly on to Antigua and switch to a LIAT flight for Beef Island on Tortola in the North Caribbean, enjoying the ease of travelling without longboards. *En route,* the plane makes two unscheduled landings – 'just to pick up some extra passengers,' says the captain over the tannoy. Zed had told me that LIAT (the main inter-Caribbean airline) is affectionately known as 'leaves island any time'. I expect a slow and errant pace of life, and adapt to the already evident erratic schedule of the airline. I am here for a surf contest (a one-design event, with everyone riding the same Surftech model of board stocked at the competition venue) – maybe the normally smooth-running, and slightly hyper, contest scene will be counterbalanced by this chopped-up rhythm. This might be a syncopated waltz, with more than a touch of Fats Waller humour and plenty of purposefully off-key passages to provide quirky colour.

I arrive on the north coast of Tortola thick with a crowd hustling for stinging barrels. I source one of the board models that everyone will compete on, and paddle out into a late evening, jostling in the line-up, to see visiting Hawaiians putting on an unmatchable show of tube riding. The sky is the colour of cayenne pepper. Looking back to land, dense forest covers steep volcanic ascents, scattered with precariously balanced homes. I ride on edge all the way to shore, and turn around to see a globetrotting Californian pulling in backside to score an extravagant lay-back barrel.

Overleaf: The band sways on – with Tristan Jenkin and Zed Layson, Bottom Bay, Barbados

The international mix of surfers steals set after set from the locals. Fortunately, they allow the pros the room to strut their stuff. But there are always the local guardians. A clean, overhead, see-through, emerald-coloured peak barrels along the reef. A visitor paddles inside and snatches it from the biggest local. 'He thinks he can snake me. He don't know the rules,' says the local. 'I normally give 'em three chances,' says a visitor, nervously. 'This ain't baseball,' the local replies – 'don't worry if you see that guy with two black eyes tomorrow; there'll be one from my right fist and one from my left.' Suddenly, a school of minnows bursts from the deep, chased by larger fish, maybe tuna, chased by something bigger. There is a frenzy of splashing, some panic. 'When you paddle out, you enter the food chain,' says the local – in other words, the take-off pecking order.

The splashing turns out to be tarpen. The sea swarms with a feeding frenzy, soon joined by an enormous gathering of dive-bombing pelicans. When the next set arrives, the surface is so torn that the barrel will be unmakeable. I am sitting deepest, and finally have a set. I take it, pull in, but the lip quivers and wavers mockingly, stalling me deeper and deeper in a bending cavern. I hang on tight, stay locked in and accelerate out of a smoking tube ride. Despite my contact lenses, I am beginning to develop some of the finer tricks of tube riding that haunted me by their absence on those early Indonesia trips.

Getting tubed and staying in the present on quick take-offs where the pitching wave can so easily pick you off, is like jumping into a solo at the peak of an arc, rather than building it up. But improvised solos do not have to be long to be sweet or stunning. A critical hang ten in an impossible spot may be over in the blink of an eye, but that compact solo can take the breath away. When John Coltrane was playing with Miles Davis, he would characteristically take off on an intense meander, soloing for 20 minutes at a time at a high level of invention. Davis used to get fed up with this, where he felt good solos could be short yet inventive. He urged Coltrane to cut the length of his solos. Coltrane said he did not know how, he just got possessed and had to play. Davis replied: 'I'll tell you how – take the motherf***ing horn out of your mouth!'

The great waves continue right through the contest. If you have to deal with crowded line-ups at world-class breaks, what better way to ease the strain than to enter a contest, where you get to surf with maybe only one other person out, as long as you keep winning heats. It is a great motivator. A benefit from competing internationally has been to enjoy empty sessions at usually crowded line-ups in places like Brazil, Mexico, South Africa, Spain, Portugal and even at home in Cornwall, while getting to know the characters along the way. Of course, I have felt jaded about contests many times, but the buzz of winning, or at least performing well, is the kind of energy that usually stays with you, because you tend to be surfing against the best in the game and that really pushes you.

After the event, I explain to some of the contest crew that I am spending my prize money on a photo project in Italy with John. 'Surf in the Mediterranean? Give me a break,' they say in disbelief. Italian friends Nik and Emi had shown me photographs of tantalizing, head-high tubes in Tuscany, Genoa and Rome. When the Mistral blows, funnelling down the Rhone Valley in France to touch the warmer Mediterranean, the waves can become exceptional on the exposed western and northern shores of Italy. They are stunningly documented in one of the best-designed European surf magazines – *SurfNews* – run by Nik in Ravenna. He explained that, while *Big Wednesday* flopped in America, a subtitled version achieved cult status in Italy, and a surf culture quickly developed in the wake of a windsurfing boom. Maybe there was some bizarre, unconscious link with spaghetti westerns. After all, John Milius' film could be read as a 'frontier' movie and a 'shoot-out' between the fading culture of post-war Californian longboarding and the new sharpshooters on the block with their Lightning Bolt shortboards. I could not wait to find out for myself, and collected a renaissance malibu to glide the Mediterranean.

On the flight to Rome, I read the late Italian poet Eugenio Montale's *The Bones of Cuttlefish*. He writes about the immensity of the sea's body, aproned with spent seaweed and starfish, as if life expired once beached. He won the Nobel Prize in 1975, and no modern Italian writer has captured the spirit of the Mediterranean as well as Montale. It reminds me of what I felt as a child, dragged back and forth in the shorebreak of my home breaks – a feeling that the sea is in me as I am in the sea. This is the twin 'plasmas' that the modernist French poet St John Perse (also a Nobel Prize winner for poetry, in 1960) describes as the salt-blood running through a person that mirrors ocean saline. The point of surfing is to challenge the sea's desire to beach you, to throw you up half-dead on the shore, throwing up. And I see this challenge as translating potential fear into a kind of jazz, improvising in tune with the sea's great movements, turning surfing into artistic statement. What better place to indulge the aesthetic of surfing than Italy?

Arriving in Rome, John and I are greeted by Emi's forecast that there will be 'three hours of 3-foot waves.' And this is precisely what we get at his local spot. Later, we eat *prosciutto* and sip *prosecco* on his spacious, grapevine-lined balcony. This has to be the most civilized surf trip I have ever been on. Nik explains that surf prediction is a different art here. Simply put – where will the longest fetch strike? This follows a long tradition of forecasting for a seafaring people. Hippocrates, writing his classic treatise on medicine 400 years BC, compares the diagnostic art of a physician with the navigational skills of a ship's pilot or rudderman, who must piece together a host of cues and clues to predict the weather and ocean conditions. As a network of surfers confirms the prediction, you have to be on your toes, prepared for a lot of travelling. Italian surfers simply accept that surfing requires movement and exploration. But, again, Mediterranean peoples are historically seafarers, at home on Homer's 'wine-dark' sea.

Statuesque pose without wave – Rome

There is a sudden and violent storm, and we can plan to surf its subsequent wave explosion in the south. But it will not be from the usually consistent Mistral, and Nik panics because the only place rideable for the next few days is apparently one of the most localized 'secret' surf breaks in Italy. Guardianship of secrets has been considered paramount in this rapidly growing, inconsistent, and thus potentially overcrowded, surf nation, so Nik spends the rest of the day negotiating with the 'boss' of the scene we hope to visit. Since it is apparently 'his' neighbourhood, we have to show some respect – and we must get formally invited. By evening Nik confirms the invitation we had hoped for. The locals shadow our every movement in a session marred by infrequent waves. I try not to steal sets – I do not want to leave with a vendetta on my head. But our grace and style win over the home crew, and we are soon accepted as welcome guests. We eat on baroque balconies in front of unique set-ups, forming new and lasting friendships, before leaving in order to chase a new swell while an intense electrical storm lights up the wide horizon.

We cross the Straits of Messina to Sicily, amid a scramble of traffic eager to ferry over before the next general strike. Look at the map – this island is the foot-

Statuesque pose with wave – Puglia

ball kicked by the soccer-crazy mainland boot. I think of my own home at the toe of Cornwall – the foot of west Britain's leg – more the foot of a rugby player than a footballer in a rugby-proud county. I think also of the violent, rapidly changing Atlantic weather that jogs back and forth along the limb of coast. Our rugby ball has long since burst, to form the various Isles of Scilly. Here, in the non-tidal Mediterranean, the football retains its shape. From inside the island there is cohesion achieved through the extraordinary binding force of 'family' (and 'honourable men'). The Mediterranean and my hometown of Penzance are inextricably linked through the ancient tradition of the tin trade, for traders collected the scarce resource of tin from Mount's Bay.

For surfers, the most heavily navigated waters on earth, around the heart of the Mediterranean, are strangely uncharted. This reinforces the stereotype that there simply cannot be waves in this sea. Such prejudices are the moat in the eye of the outsider. Such moats are familiar to any British surfer. Californians, asked in the early 1960s about surf in Britain, would laugh at such an idea. An infamous Rick Griffin cartoon article written by Ron Stoner in *Surfer* magazine lampooned 'surfing in the United Kingdom' as foggy 'London' with its beefeaters and bowler

Water music wherever you go
Tiles meet styles– Siracusa, Sicily

hats and 'Scotland' with its castles. In fact, the article was written without the visit ever being made – it was fiction. They simply penned it from the office, never bothered to make the trip, and produced a string of amusing stereotypes. I still meet people today who are astounded at the vibrant British surf scene and its high standards. I have a feeling Sicily will deliver in the same mould.

A south-east fetch translates into long, head-high reeling lefts at Capo Punto. The best peelers of our expedition unfold across waters with a yellow-green glaze like olive oil. A local surfer appears in a Fiat 126, anxious to make the most of the rare conditions. There are characters in every spot. This Italian local, with his salt-stained, bronzed curls and red beard, looks like he has taken the part of a Roman god acting at the Teatro Greco in Syracuse. He paddles out, looping between Nik, Emi and me, disregarding our orderly system to take waves in turn. 'I know how it works,' he says, 'but since you guys surf more than me, I deserve more waves. And since my spot only works six times a year, when it breaks, there are no universal rules.' We accede to local rules.

Wary at first, I get to know this guy a little better. I find he has an intriguing history, a pedigree. He happened to be the first surfer on this stretch of Sicily's coast, the lone local. He was a social outcast, who turned down the chance to be an orthodontist in the city to follow in the wake of his father – making a living fishing and diving. His whole surfing evolution has been totally instinctive, like his understanding of the ocean, and he has framed surfing entirely in terms of fishing. He says, with great sincerity, that when it became a cult hit in Italy he watched *Big Wednesday* and was instantly inspired. He felt he could do what those characters in the film were doing. Since I too was motivated by that movie, I readily understand his enthusiasm. He explains that he used 'Japanese fishing rope to stop his board from tumbling on the rocks.' For the bigger days, when his 'heart beats faster,' he has a board with a 'rounded stern for the deeper troughs.' The translation from boat to board is interesting. The fishing mindset helps in the local context, where most Mediterranean surfing is weather-watching and forecasting. 'When people want the sea to rise, it does,' he says, with more than a little hubris. His surf philosophy is that good waves come to the people who deserve them, and the people who deserve them are the ones who respect the break. The tradition remains unbroken – always respect the gods, especially the spirits of place. I get to like this guy and his homespun philosophy.

We have two days left in the Mediterranean. Checking the cloudy sky, John notices that the wind has ceased and that soon it will be flat. We surf the last hour of swell, getting the most from every dropping peak. I think about what the local said – the world gives back to those who respect it. We still need a sunny session to get some good photographs from the trip. I am in perfect position on the take-off, but leave the choice set wave to a grateful Sicilian local. Contrary to the forecast, on the next and last morning the sky clears and we all surf a totally new and unexpected swell in bright sun. The gods favour us. The sea turns from ink-blue to almost purple, the colour of robust red wine, a hearty Barolo from Piedmont, each wave savoured by thirsty surfers drunk on Italian swell. All that 'panamania' paid off as I learned to see through the label to taste the wine in the bottle. Never trust a stereotype, and try not to caricature. Surf in the Mediterranean? Another glass, please.

9 Buddha on Board

Scanning the horizon off Hainan Island, China's southernmost province, my senses are suddenly drawn landward. Sitting serene, up from the beach, elevated on a pyramid of steps, is a huge golden Buddha. This is a remarkable sight – a 1,600-year-old survivor from the Tang Dynasty, the Mahajana School. In Communist China, Buddhism is effectively outlawed. Yet here, on the southerly fringe, juniper smoke snakes into the air from a dusty shrine scattered with incense sticks and jade. In his own time, the Buddha himself would surely have created this kind of embarrassment for the dominant regime. I turn back to face the sea, take off late and am soon wrapped in an iridescent curtain. I glance up at the Buddha glancing down. While the conditions are not the best I have surfed, this Buddha-moment is one of supreme grace. I paddle out charged with the present. If I understand Buddhism correctly, living fully in the present in a sense eradicates time, for there is no mindless wandering to recollection, and no fruitless future guesswork. This state of mind is when you perform at your best, not mindless, but mindful. The ancient Chinese beliefs of Confucianism, Taoism and Buddhism are often brought together in a syncretic appreciation of nature, suggesting, perhaps, that if you respect the wave and its life-form, you get the best out of the ride.

Staying in the present is one of the most important things that I am learning from travel. Paradoxically, planning a trip means thinking ahead the whole time, and a surf trip puts emphasis on this as you spend a lot of time putting together clues as to where the best breaks may be. But within this general frame of preparedness, the rule is to stick with the now. Again, jazz can teach so much about this. Charlie Parker's much covered tune 'Now's the Time' is about improvisation in the present. The joke runs: 'What is the time?' The response: 'Now is the time'! Those who make improvisation in the present look easy are thinking ahead, but confidently drawing this knowledge into the here-and-now.

After the surf, I visit the Buddha temple up-close with John. The keeper returns to the shrine at the base of the steps with fresh fish and coconuts. Old world meets new, as he sets up to chop open a coconut, machete held back, and then drops the blade as his mobile phone rings! When did the practised arc of the machete on coconut husk come to mix with the now ubiquitous ringtone? In some ways, this mirrors the mix of Buddhism and Communism. And we bring contemporary surfing to add to the ancient sea-lore of the local fishing community. Nowhere in the world, apart from India, is the past being eclipsed so quickly by the present as in China. But how can a history as rich as China's simply be

Don't look back – Hainan Island, Chin

erased? It was Marx who insisted that the political present cannot be understood without recourse to history, yet Mao's brand of Communism attempted to erase history to enforce his own vision of the present, including wiping out the Buddhist legacy and its Tibetan focus, deliberately destroying China's antiquity.

It is getting dark and we have to find a place to stay. We drive back up the overgrown, red-sand track to the road, back-dropped by the Lima mountains, wondering if we will have to go as far as Haikou to eat and sleep. We pass bicyclists and tricyclists, and snatch snippets of action leaking from rickety bamboo shacks. I see a wise, old weathered face, not craggy but soft like silk, looking intently not at the person opposite him, as locals play cards, but politely at the ground. Communication is without direct eye contact, through glance, allusion, the sideways gesture. The Chinese psyche is not about confrontation, but about hint, glancing off something rather than going to it directly, the sinuous movement. They are sipping rice wine and do not look up. We seem to go unnoticed, despite the unnatural rack of boards on the roof. But, of course, we are noticed, and acknowledged, with the effortless use of the corner of the eye.

Waxing up, looking down – Hainan, China

I see out of the corner of my eye a sign written in English – Haiseng Resort in Long Lou. Potluck. It turns out that a Malaysian-Chinese hotel tycoon owns the place and speaks excellent English. Overwhelmed to see foreign visitors, he treats us to a feast. The small sip of *chi*, served in delicate porcelain, is a quintessential experience. The Chinese obsession with taste is set out before us – pure, clean, contrasting flavours. Delicate portions of noodle soup, garlic-fried spinach leaf, Wenchang boiled chicken, pig's stomach, crab, beef, spicy chilli tofu, lychee, star fruit and finally, butter-fried coffee beans. You do not just think the philosophy of Tao, the balance of forces, you taste it.

We explore a coast blanketed by rainforest, consulting a sea chart and a barely legible local map. Where the roads turn to fine dirt, a few motorbikes sputter, chickens make tired squawks, and families of agile macaque monkeys swing past. We surf frisky beachbreaks, then take shade beneath driftwood fishing huts. But the unforgettable hours are under the watchful eye of the Buddha, surfing in the present, like Ornette Coleman's melodic fusions of Chinese, Malian and Indian music played against variations of rock rhythms.

What a shoc

We try sugarcane with the keeper of the temple, and our vocabulary quickly expands to encompass the bare essentials – *Ni hao, Xie xie* and *Zai jian*. We try to interact with more of the locals. Loud and pushy, smoking and spitting, with loud voices, they seem brash at first and out of kilter with those quiet card players. But I begin to admire their unwavering focus on the present. They are calm and assured, rarely blinking at anything unusual. Expressing astonishment is impolite.

The wind swell dissolves, so we hire a driver to explore the far north of the island. He blows his horn through every village, and in synchrony overtaking every bike. We crawl through the steamy regional capital, Haikou, the streets choked with traffic and the babble of commerce. It is pleasantly shabby, and I note the fashion for facing new buildings in bathroom tiles. Three forces meet in China: an overwhelming urge for Westernization – clothes, fast food, punk music and a craze for Japanese motorbikes – mixed with tradition (or the reinvention of tradition), and the still powerful grip of state socialism. The prospective has replaced the retrospective. China is turning from history to anticipation, signalling a massive cultural shift. But rapid industrialization, and now the post-industrial development

of international-style cities, has been bought at the cost of escalating pollution, where smog-shrouded Beijing resembles nineteenth-century London.

As the global world first emerged in the seventeenth century, European traders sought a shortened sea route to China. For all the stories of the greed for gold that led to Spanish conquest in the Americas, the canny traders knew that the best way to get cheap gold was to export silver (obtained for next to nothing, mainly in Peru) to China. Where 12 units of silver were needed in Europe to buy one unit of gold, in China, only six units were needed. Paradoxically, the world trade market, including the importation of exquisite porcelain from China to Europe, was opened up through three Chinese inventions – the compass, paper and gunpowder. The compass revolutionized sea voyages; paper meant that permanent records could be kept of transactions; and gunpowder used in firearms allowed Europeans to subjugate the native Americans around the Great Lakes in Canada, which acted as the base for the opening of trade routes from the Atlantic to Hudson Bay. This was thought to be the short route to China. The fabled wealth of Asia, of which the European nations wanted a slice, was the lure that led to the first global wave of European colonialism in the seventeenth century.

Walking along the empty beach at the northernmost point of Hanain Island, I feel again the tremendous sense of lost history, masked by the ugly remains of recent conflict. There is little potential for surf – just open coast, the swell swallowed by the shallow shelf of the Qiongzhou Strait across to the mainland. Lines of abandoned, dilapidated concrete army bunkers, old defences, reach as far as the gunmetal water. Isolationism has been a central feature in Chinese history from the Ming Dynasty's Great Wall – a grandiose but futile attempt to stem the invasion of the northern tribes – to Mao's vision of rural development, where urban intellectuals were banished to the countryside to rediscover 'true social values'.

Heading back south to surf the usual spots we arrive just as school has finished, and a fleet of kids are peddling past with bamboo garden rakes trailing from the tails of their bicycles. Most seem oblivious to our presence – as if they want to notice, but know they should not, offering just a hint of recognition, the subtle glance, the quick sideways look. Staring is impolite. The waves are small, and I manage to encourage some of them to have a go at surfing. When you do this, ownership of the board often becomes the chief focus. But with the Hainan kids, patience is master. They take turns, all quickly mastering a clean ride. The Chinese have always produced great athletes. Natural balance for sure, the yin and yang in revolution, a still centre. China's two conflicting traditions, Confucianism and Taoism, remain in dialogue even within state socialism. Confucianism is about the polite and obedient citizen; Taoism is about a return to the rhythms and

Left: Don't look sideways – Hainan schoolchildren

The Buddha is where you find him – Hainan, China

presences of nature, typified by the wild 'mountain man' in solitary retreat and contemplation. For decades, Maoist authorities derided both traditions as feudal superstition, but it seems that Taoism and Confucianism are indelibly imprinted on the population, as complementary expressions of the raw and the cooked, nature and culture. Confucius suggested that perfect balance is reflected in calm water, a model for composure. This is the social instinct – polite compromise. At the heart of Taoism is a paradoxical wild calm. Nature is a vortex and you are at its eye, involved but not involved. We are back to the twin essences of surfing, the tube ride and the noseride: both require absolute poise, calm, and a kind of withdrawal at the eye of the vortex.

The kids ride my latest Town and Country (T&C) epoxy longboard. It uses the yin and yang symbol as its emblem. A Hawaii-perfected model repackaged as a high-performance, Asian-made, postmodern board that pops out of a factory mould. This lightweight but robust, travel-friendly type of board has evolved during my two decades of commercial involvement with surfing. When I was the

Balance through motion – Cheyne Cottrell, aerial

same age as these kids, all I knew of yin and yang was the Hawaiian surfboard label T&C – such is the power of surf marketing. T&C's groundbreaking test pilots were among the loosest, futuristic surfers in history – Larry 'Rubberman' Bertlemann and Dane Kealoha in the 1970s (progressing Gerry Lopez's fluid Hawaiian style), and Martin 'Pottz' Potter in the 1980s. Balance through extreme motion became their trademark.

Radical, low-carving Hawaiian Bertlemann inspired a new, progressive Californian skateboarding style in the mid-1970s, termed 'Dogtown' for its spawning-ground near the derelict neighbourhoods of Venice Beach. Nearly a decade later, skateboarder Rodney Mullen from Florida perfected the flat-ground 'ollie' by flicking into the air. Californian surfers took this scalding skateboard manoeuvre into the water. The outcome was the aerial, soon at the cutting edge of surfing. British-born Pottz and Californians Christian Fletcher and Matt Archibold launched

Overleaf: No room for squares – American Tom Curren at Pipeline

their careers by perfecting their aerial repertoires. Pottz pushed the limits with raw power, deep carves and startling, rail-burying turns. His airborne cover shot on *Surfing* magazine in 1984, and the abilities of Tom Curren, Tom Carroll and Mark Occhilupo, would inspire the Momentum generation of the 1990s. Taylor Steele's Momentum videos showcased a group of Americans spearheaded by Kelly Slater, Rob Machado and Shane Dorian, eclipsing the power surfers who went before them with previously unseen acrobatics to a high-octane California-punk soundtrack. This digression into surf history is important, because in many ways the longboard renaissance, involving younger surfers, acted as a backlash to the Momentum movement, which was all about in-your-face surfing. And here in China, I discover that the art of communication, whether person-to-person, or kids first trying longboarding, is the opposite of in-your-face. It is the indirect glance off something that matters, not the direct hit. We see this as 'politeness', but it is manners of another sort. It is a graceful and intricate way of communicating, crab-like, sideways, indirect.

The eccentric and talented Australian Peter Drouyn (recently publicly declaring his wish for transsexual identity shift) explored the south-east coast of China in the early 1970s. Despite his fabulous tales of great surf, Drouyn took no photographer, and so had no evidence, and was soon eclipsed by Alby Falzon's 'discovery' of Bali's wave force. Drouyn, an Asian studies graduate, revisited China in 1985, when he found waves here on Hainan Island. Typically flamboyant, he attempted to persuade the Chinese government to hire him as coach of their future national surf team. He was convinced that surfing would be an Olympic sport, and that Chinese surfers could become world champions. But the government refused Drouyn a visa extension, perhaps because he was too direct, and he returned to Australia empty-handed.

Surf commercialism has yet to greet these kids. But the world knows that the future market is China, as nearly one-sixth of the globe's population. Think of the huge potential in areas like Shanghai, a megalopolis twice the size of California, spread along the Yangtze river delta like a cement, steel and concrete dragon. Waves are close – in fact 'Shanghai' means 'on the sea'. Maybe Taoism could be a template for the emergence of surfing – balancing the opposites of town and country.

That night, we have the spectacle of a clear, waxing, almost-full moon, accompanied by rust-red Mars. My developing image of the local Chinese as a mix of the politeness of Confucianism and the acceptance of the often tangled disorder of nature central to the 'mountain men' Taoists may be a stereotype, but I am beginning to see its manifestation – its archetype. We drive to Sanya City, the southern tip of Hainan Island, where a hotel tourism boom has gripped a dour fishing port. We head straight for the old wharf, through back alleys filled with rundown tea-houses. Here is the home of the mountain men and women. We wander through the harbour quarter, and the pier is packed with scantily clad ladies of the night and their male customers. The beach is close by, but offers further disappointment, as touts aggressively trying to sell trinkets mob us. To add to the strange cultural mix, Muslim Hui women (Vietnamese refugees from the old maritime silk road) sell pearl necklaces and betel-nut (*binlang*), which is cultivated as a stimulant. Red spit marks the sand. Just about everyone in this neighbourhood has bright-coloured lips and teeth, as they chew slices of the palm seed wrapped inside a heart-shaped pepper-vine leaf. The betel-nut offers a sharp, short hit, leaving twin stains – a dye on the skin, and a lifetime habit.

After the tranquillity of the east coast, Sanya is 'Sin City', and a shock to the system. Faux-tourist leisure-land meets the golden sand, presenting another dilemma – the uneasy mix of state Communism and global moneymaking. Waikiki is due east, so Sanya has become known as 'The Oriental Hawaii'. Jet-planed in from the frozen north, splashing in the shallows, the hordes of Chinese tourists seem strangely uneasy with beach life. But Sanya actually has the best surf set-ups we have seen on the island – a collection of quality reefs that could unleash on a typhoon swell. Unfortunately, the most impressive-looking right-hander will soon vanish like the rest of local history, lost to pier development. Given that state Communism promises shared ownership, access to the coast is, paradoxically, increasingly modelled on the idea of private privilege.

In Nanshan coastal beauty spot we pay to see the sea – a few smoothly weathered granite cupolas packaged as a 'natural' experience. We have spent more cash here in a few days than in the previous two weeks on the east coast. Troops of holidaymakers are ferried about with the tour guide, wearing bright dragon-print attire, flip-up Chips shades and Panama-Jack hats. The highlight of this experience is certainly the way out, when we are chaperoned through a well-stocked sweet shop; counters of cosmetics; a stack of once-colourful fashion posters, now faded into sickly shades; past the garment rails, and out into the waiting trinket hawkers, desperate for trade. What a bizarre ride! Disneyland-China on *binlang*. I am reminded that at my home, on one of the most beautiful stretches of coastline in the world, is The Land's End Experience, where the most westerly tip of Britain ('next stop New York!') has been turned into a tourist 'experience'. Not much different really from Nanshan or Coney Island. As a number of contemporary cultural commentators have noted, the global experience is now a 'Coney Island of the mind', as we are all plugged into an expectation that global life will be a theme park with recognizable features – McDonalds, Coca Cola, Nike. What would those seventeenth-century explorers who were seeking the passage to China think of the 'Disneyfication' of the world?

We arrive at a new hotel, impressed by the extravagant décor, the outdoor gymnasium, and the firework display for 'moon-cake night', a lunar celebration. But this is all a façade, hiding the realities of a horrendously (mis)managed insti-

Balance with motion – tube ride

tution intent on fleecing us. '*Deposuie insufficient – pledge money*' reads a mis-spelt note that the overstaffed hotel sends back after I sign the tab for our meal. Obviously we cannot keep a room tab here, so we pay up in cash there and then. Job done? No. They demand, 'You pay bill. Or we will lock room.' What bill? We have paid for everything, every step of the way so far for four days, waiting for a swell. It takes us an hour to smooth it out. And then the same thing happens in the morning as we attempt to check out. We guess that the staff members have been pocketing the cash we have paid, and the management has no idea. This is capitalism of the worst sort, obscuring the best values of Maoism, such as collective responsibility, care for your neighbour, and common ownership of the means of production.

My mood lightens when I experiment with the outdoor gymnasium facilities just before we leave to drive eight hours north and fly out of Haikou. I am intrigued by some of the obscure, slightly goofy-looking contraptions, but they turn out to be hilariously useless devices: a 'cross-trainer' for running that keeps my knees perfectly straight, while my arms are hurled out-and-in on curved handlebars at 90 degrees to my leg swing. The 'cycling machine' lifts me up and forwards every time I peddle, practically launching me off the object, as if I have jammed on the front brakes. Post-breakfast workout in *binlang*.

I would love to travel again to China to sample its spectacular inland scenery, vibrant visual arts, exciting contemporary writers, and to better understand the paradoxes of its culture. But our trip left me with mixed feelings. I have flown out of places with a good taste, where the surf did not work out too well but the cultural experience was rich. Leaving China's south coast I felt uneasy about the movement from a revered golden Buddha to seaside trinket-hawkers; from the elegance of the meaningful sideways glance to the faceless rip-off hotel. I was missing the feeling of flow, the sense of the unexpected, the beauty of improvisation. Mao's cultural revolution saw jazz as a Western indulgence, but this forgets that jazz was born from worksong suffered in black slavery, and is music signalling liberation from oppression. The Nazis banned jazz as it was seen as a wild Black, Jewish and Gypsy music, where militaristic marching music was preferred. China's soul surely honours wonder, the unexpected, the improvised and the Zen paradox.

Some jazz musicians play so much from the heart that their music hits you like a bullet. If it hits you like a sledgehammer, something is wrong, because then the music dulls or knocks you senseless. You want the music to be killer, so that you can be reborn in its presence. Some *avant-garde*, free jazz players are all about noise, but who needs more noise in their lives? Players like the tenor sax geniuses John Coltrane and David Murray play with a big tone that is also intense, pushing away at the changes, playing every possible sequence of notes to wring the last ounce of change out of a tune. When Larry Bertlemann first came on the scene, people called him 'Rubberman' because he put himself in such impossible situations all the time – always on an edge, carving an impossible turn, working against the grain, milking every possible ounce of speed to set up for a blast through a normally unmakeable section. Bertleman could jam on the tail, letting everything suddenly reel on, only to step on the gas and chase down the drummer with howling runs, hollering the history of jazz as call-and-response slave song, letting freedom ring. If you could can intensity in surfing, Bertlemann would be the top brand. But this was 'soul' surfing in the same way that Coltrane's music was devotional outpouring. He could not stop playing a solo because there was no end to the road. Occasionally, you get genius surfers who show both John Coltrane's intensity and Miles Davis' open phrasing together – like Kelly Slater, Laird Hamilton and Joel Tudor. There was a good reason that Davis invited Coltrane to be the tenor sax player in his first great quintet. Too much intensity is overwhelming, too much space is underwhelming. Put the two together and you have a great combination as band and as surfer. Next stop – Korea.

10 Confronting the Kimchi

My first glimpse of South Korean culture is the hypermodern, automated cleaning cart, polishing floors in Seoul's Incheon Airport. It zips past, and I take a beeline to the water fountain, struck by an insatiable thirst, aggravated by the air-conditioning. The water-fountain, inevitably, is electronic, so I wave my palms until I trigger a frustratingly low spout, and then eagerly start to drink. I shuffle my feet slightly and accidentally set off another function, and it jet-washes my forehead. My flight is called, I run past a concentration of advertisements for 'Enchanting Jeju' and 'Honeymoon Island', and strap into yet another plane, happy to leave the hi-tech concrete canyons of 'automated' Seoul for Jeju City in the East China Sea.

John, Randy, Emi and I arrive to greet an intense rainstorm and a perplexing language barrier. It takes a gentle stubbornness, some persuasive smiles, and a whole range of air-wrestling hand gestures to load our mass of boards on to the coach bound for the south coast tourist quarter. Jungmun beach has the best exposure on the coast to hot-water typhoon swells between August and October, but the surrounding hotels prove too expensive, so we find a cheaper, and charming, *minbak* in humble Sinsuseong Town.

In the morning, the extreme, stair-rod rainstorm has passed, and a sight of the sea confirms that Jeju has excellent waves. South Korea is a place more associated with Samsung, Hyundai and taekwondo than surf. But here at Jungmun, a left point, a right reef, and a safer beachbreak meet as one, before unpacking in a brutal shorebreak on sheets of black mica sand, raked as the foam apron rushes up and sucks back. The curvaceous right is operating like a pressure cooker, trapping air and spitting it back out. We drop into inviting tubes with a liability clause – a buoy-lined swimming area, over which we have to ollie, like skateboarders, every time we connect to the inside. Otherwise, we get snagged by the buoys' connecting rope.

As the day ripens, the landscape gives off a wonderful scent – tangerine groves above the basalt cliffs that drop away to meet cola-coloured boulders rained on by a stunning waterfall. Developers have spotted this beautiful landscape with a strange mix of hotels, windmills, bridges and cherry-roofed conference centres that perversely turn their backs on the sea view, perhaps to emphasize the work ethic over play. By 10 a.m. the lifeguards are on duty, and a similarly perverse scene is developing on the beach. Pasty-skinned honeymooners hire yellow rubber rings, wade out of their collective depths, then get annihilated by the sea's sounding board that is a pummelling shorebreak. The chain-smoking lifeguards zealously guard the buoy-line. It is the only place in the whole bay they have to keep safe.

Looking for an angle – Randy Rarick, Jungmun

The trouble is, the lively end-section of the right-hander streams through this area. I am jet-washed from a tube, straight over the zone, and the lifeguards scare the living daylights out of me, unleashing a monster-decibel air-raid siren.

Two locals paddle out, but the overhead sections are challenging for them. They cling to the shoulder, wide-eyed, and we keep an eye out for their safety. After the session, they take us to the local pharmacy in Sinsuseong Town, where they both work. This is also the social hangout for the nascent Jeju surf community. They recently formed the Wave Club, after they caught the bug from some visiting Japanese surfers. We consume excessive quantities of fibre-filled, vitamin-rich, sugary health tonics from medicinal-looking 100ml glass bottles, and go online to check the forecast – an increasing swell.

My senses are hyper-alert for the afternoon session, after another power drink and a huge gulp of Pocari Sweat, a clear fluid that I thought was mineral water, but turns out to be a vile-tasting iron replacement isotonic. With this much glucose in my blood, I am furious when the Jungmun lifeguards declare 'No surfing!' across the PA, refusing to let us paddle out. The swell has tripled in size since the morning. With the beach closed, we do not want to offend the lifeguards, and

On Green Dolphin Street – Jungmun

opt to ride the left point, out of their sight. Following a tricky walk across slippery rocks, I deal with an astonishing fifteen-wave closeout set. Pacific typhoon swells are famous for long lulls and chronically overloaded sets.

We claw further and further outback. After heavy rainfall, the water is pea-green and detritus has littered the line-up. Randy has to turn a regulation duck-dive underneath a breaking lip into a full roll when he sees a huge log thundering towards him. Thankfully, it just misses his head. Noting that Randy's board has a hefty chunk missing from the rail, we are now alert not only to hair-raising lips spending their force on our heads, but also to the floating log torpedoes that might be catapulted forward in them. To our amazement, one of the locals paddles out. At the pharmacy, I marked this guy as the town joker, pulling wheelies on his moped. Heart visibly thumping, he scrambles to avoid getting mauled by what are almost certainly the biggest waves he has ever attempted to surf. I guess one of those original Japanese visitors must have been surfing two-foot-high noon sessions wearing a hat, because he still has his on backwards, in imitation, as if this would be a lucky charm against the sea's force. The set sweeps it clean away. He turns shoreward to grab it, while we are more concerned about the coming closeout slamming him into the rocks. Luckily, the hat floats, and half an hour later, with some encouragement and support from us, he snags two sizeable waves and, remarkably, never loses hold of his prize trucker cap. Perhaps it is a genuine good luck charm.

After a testing session, paddling in offers little choice but to use the beach, closed to surfing, as a safe exit, risking the wrath of the lifeguards. Emi and Randy get a warning whistle, but I manage to veer west, just in front of the forbidden roped zone. As I stand up on a hurtling, hollow right to take me to the shorebreak ensemble, I hear the siren once again. I walk past the lifeguards with a coy, apologetic wave. Later, we all have a laugh about the confrontation over a cold glass of Hite beer, recalling the ear-piercing sound and the perplexed look on the lifeguards' faces. Right now, maintaining a long-standing tradition, competent surfers and zealous lifeguards will be at loggerheads at some beach or other across the globe. The archetypal confrontation between authority and freedom, played out between the characters in *Big Wednesday*, is as much a part of the surfing life as your sinuses emptying inappropriately at a black-tie evening function, when you had been surfing all afternoon with some heavy hold-downs.

The local brew is a letdown, and will not offer a memory stimulated by Randy's collection of obscure beer labels from around the globe. The beer says 'made from naturally fresh spring water' on the label, and tastes pretty much true to the description, advertising a distinct lack of hops. The food, however, is potent, and the Hite then becomes a good counterpoise. Hot *kimchi* fizzes in my throat, and leaves a curious taste, spicy and sour. The fermented and pickled vegetables were once made to preserve nutrients during harsh northern winters. Now *kimchi* is an essential part of every Korean meal, even in the south. We are introduced to an amazing range of dishes, where *kimchi* are accompanied by *heukdwaeji bulgogi* (black pork), *haemuljeongol* (seafood stew), and *hoe* (raw fish). We cook the meat ourselves over a white-hot stone and grill in a deep hole in the middle of a low table. I am grateful that we have met the Wave Club crew. Without culinary guidance, who knows what mystery meat you will unknowingly eat here? 'Duck' is pronounced with an 'aw' sound, 'dawk', and since there is no difference in pronunciation between 'G' and 'K', dog sounds like 'dawk', and the Korean word for 'chicken' is *dak*. Culinary vigilance is the watchword for any less adventurous eaters. I round things off with *sujeongwa* (cinnamon and ginger tea), and mentally start dealing with the promise of the largest swell I have seen all year.

The typhoon surf starts to close out the whole of Jungmun, so while the local surfers are buckling down to work in Sinsuseong Town, we hire a driver, Jung, and his shiny new Hyundai van. Jung does not speak any English and we have no Korean between us, so there is a long lag between our requests and his responses, which leads to many missed turnings on the road. Lost in translation becomes just plain 'lost'. Before we master any Korean, Jung perfects 'beach', but pronounces it with an 'ey' on the end. Every turning becomes 'beachey?' It is never easy educating a first-timer in the ways of surf exploration. We can be seen as

Overleaf: Setting up for the solo – Jumgmun

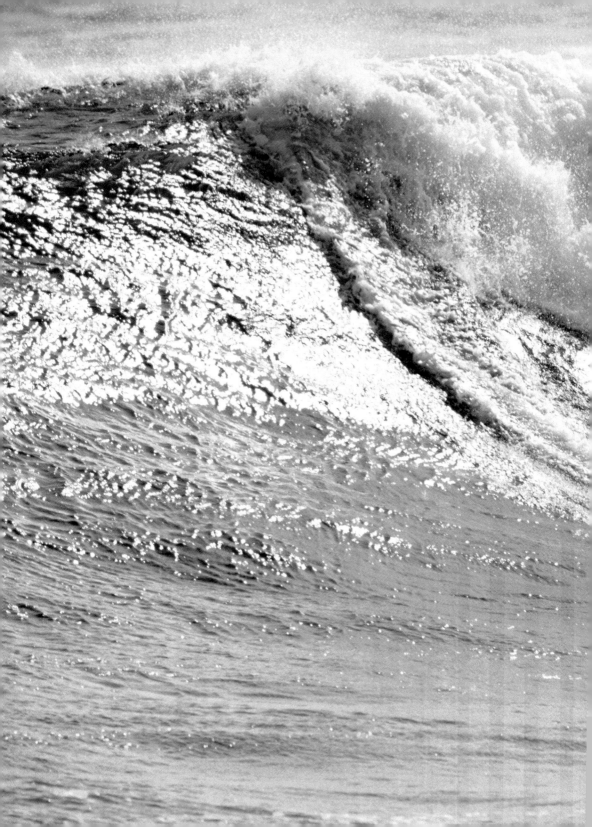

the product of an affluent culture with too much time on our hands. Typically, we search every escarpment and cove, beach and bay, cliff and harbour along the south coast between Songaksan and Pyoseon, only to head right back to the first spot we checked close to Jungmun. At Dombenanggol, a boulder-strewn cove has a cracking short right, with a hairy take-off. The local fishermen try to call us ashore, shouting what we learn later is 'danger!' in Korean, not just to save us from drowning, but to prevent us from damaging their precious mussel beds. As the tide rises, the shallow left gets longer, and we switch over for some fast rides over a sharp bottom, and come in, local mussels intact.

South Korea is a wired society of hardworking, serious and motivated people, based on an economic miracle, self-styled as 'a dragon that rose from the ditch'. In the Confucian mould, conventional etiquette embodies strict hierarchy, so that everybody knows how to behave and speak with respect towards each other. Status and dignity are very important. Throw some Tao-infested T&C surf tourists into the Confucian code and Koreans are totally baffled. Most are quite simply lost for words, because they do not want to offend us. This attitude leaves little room for a frivolous pursuit like surfing. But in thriving South Korea, new things can attract the young and surfing may take a hold. Jung seems increasingly curious about surfing, warming to our character, and the following morning is keen to go and explore. The whole south coast is howling onshore, so we opt to search up the west side. Despite the recent tourist boom in the south, the oval island is mostly a place of squid fishing and fruit farming. Jeju is literally translated as 'insignificant faraway province'. At Songakon, I see a fist-sized spider in a car-sized web, and cautiously peer over a 100-metre vertical cliff. We need no universal mother tongue to breathe in this staggering view. The break below also looks impressive – a deep, sheltered bay with potential minute-long lefts. However, it is inaccessible. A forty-minute walk along the beach north of the wave will be our only access, yet the tide is high, so the route is cut off for three more hours.

We head back to the snow-white van. It is stuck in black, swampy farmland. With razor-edge chino creases, starch-white shirt and crocodile-skin shoes, Jung is not dressed for adventure, but for the golf course. He contemplates what to do as aggressive mosquitoes attack me. Instinctively, I grab the keys, start up and rev the engine, spin and slide the van to safety, while splattering it, and everyone else, with muck. Jung looks at me with disguised contempt. I smile back, and suggest that we head further up the coast while the light is good. We drive past disguised, and now disused, aeroplane bunkers and army outposts built in fear of invasion from North Korea. While a new cultural wind blew through the capitalist south, the north of the peninsula became frozen in the totalitarian straightjacket of Cold War 1980, where the mysterious dictator is still believed to control the weather, and his father, dead for over a decade, remains head of state. I think of that fist-sized spider, queen of the web of her own making.

Ringing the highhat – Emi Cataldi, Chagwido

At Hama, there is an empty harbour built with ugly, five-ton tetra-pods, and a small left runs towards its exposed side. Despite our efforts, it proves too shallow, and we paddle in with dinged boards, sure that there will be a better break further north. Our judgement is good, and at Dangansanbong village next to Chagwido Island, there is a marvellous left-hander. The harbour is lined with squid drying in the sun, and a 5-foot left racks across the rock armour, sheltered from the strong east wind. Elevator-drop take-offs are followed by fast-performance turns where precise timing is essential. When the wave gets a little busy on you, drawn-out floaters slow things down, and off-the-lips are landed as if at the eye of the storm, in a still patch of ocean, the movie reel flicking over, the screen gone white. We finally put on a show for Jung, and he is suitably impressed with our chosen alternative to the golf course. Between sets, I stare out towards the village, seeing squid hung out to dry like laundry. I think of stories I have heard from Pacific fishermen about 50-foot squid with eyes like dinner plates, and the water seems more alive with sea-life, the nutrients stirred by the storm and surfacing. I suddenly feel unwelcome out there.

Jung arrives early the next morning, transformed: a sun hat, loose cotton T-shirt, shorts – adventure attire, a new identity. The internet forecasts onshore local winds for the next few days, then offshore on the south coast when a new super-typhoon swell peaks. Some of the Wave Club crew jump in, and we continue our tour of the 120-mile island. We pass the long lava caves spawned from the porous basalt of the Hallasen volcano, and watch the infamous sixty-year-old Haenyeo diving women who go as deep as 20 metres with no scuba gear, for seaweed, shellfish and sea urchins. We check every conceivable beach, reef and coastal highpoint, and map five good new reefs, far more exciting than the beachbreaks the locals had previously considered Jeju's choice surfing terrain. We make it just in time for a well-earned evening session at Chagwido. The Wave Club members take on the lefts kamikaze-style, fuelled by dangerous quantities of energy tonics, with rising lips tapping them on the shoulder out of curiosity, but not breaking their backs because they are learning to ride with speed and timing.

Speed is essential to surfing. It is about confidence and rapid decision, positioning, getting in the pocket, but also using the body as a motor, making your way into the sweet spot rather than waiting for it to happen. Nobody does speed well unless they have practised over and over, but also their physical prowess must be matched by a mental agility. The fastest sax and trumpet players – Charlie Parker, Sonny Stitt, Phil Woods, Johnny Griffin, Dizzy Gillespie, Freddie Hubbard – were also quick thinkers. The paradox about speed in surfing is that, where you need it most, in tube-riding, slotting in and making it out the other end, or at the tipping lip of a big wave drop, time also slows down.

After a crisp dawn session at Chagwido, riding the beginning of the new super-typhoon swell, we energize with an early lunch. I eat some severely hot *kimchi*. We have had our fair share of heated moments riding ledges and boils, sliding long left points, and eating strange food on this trip, but this meticulously prepared spicy *kimchi* takes the biscuit. And I begin to like it, taking more lip-stinging hits. The stuff is still fizzing in my throat when we leave. Over the next hour, the wind swings offshore along the whole southern coast, and an enormous right is breaking far out beyond the east side of Jungmun beach, all the way into the tetra-pod harbour entrance. We drive around, and the whole Wave Club crew are lining the quay in anticipation.

There is no more time to let the *kimchi* settle. The spice must now show in displays of courage and hot surfing. Randy, inevitably, is first out to taste the larger stuff. He hurtles down a mammoth face on his magenta big-wave, gun-shaped board. It looks more like the North Shore of Oahu than the East China Sea. Heart pumping hard, I paddle like lightning to the deep channel to avoid the next wave in the set cracking me on the head. I glance back to the tangerine groves that sprawl towards the sea to check my line-up marker and catch a screamer. Randy is back out and into another cascade, blaring down the wall and cranking a billowing bottom-turn, followed by a classy hook under the lip and then a poised stall before he gracefully steps forward to pull into a menacing-looking tube. Emi follows suit, also comfortable with the size from a number of trips to Hawaii, trimming at triple time as if on a piece of elastic drawn to breaking point, then

Left: Jeju Island 'grandfather' stone. Right: Temples – Mount Sanbangsan, Jeju

just making the shoulder with a flourish of cymbals over the rock bottom. Bigger waves, larger faces, give surfers the opportunity to carve big turns like snowboarders on steep, open runs – except that surfers have to cope with a moving and unpredictable surface. It is the quality of improvisation against this fast-moving pulse of the ocean as it races to dump its energy that always makes me think of surfers as kinds of jazz musicians.

The next three hours are the highlight of my surfing time in Asia. A Korean bolt from the blue – and we all score, with John getting some remarkable magazine spreads. We travelled with an openness to engage, gave something back, and reaped the rewards. We gained the respect and friendship of the Wave Club members, and opened their eyes to new waves; and they opened ours to great food, and, of course, the body-blanket that is *kimchi*. If food were matched to mood, then this addictive hot stuff would be courage. After the session, Jung, who has diligently acted as our tour guide, driver, and gracious host, summarizes what he has seen. We manage to make sense of it, as he now has some basic English, and we have a few words of Korean, and together we have a translation dictionary. 'Sam-san,' he says, 'surfing is full of beauty.' I cannot argue with that. South Korea has delivered on all fronts in a beautiful manner. It is a brilliant corner of the surfing world, offering quirky solos in the style of Thelonius Monk, with strange melodies and discords that nevertheless seem to add up. (And since we visited, a Korean Surfing Federation has formed on the mainland.)

11 Desert Blues

Jazz has its roots in the Blues, African chants transplanted to the southern states of America through the slave trade and morphed as call and response field hollers. Translated into the sacred and the profane – church music as gospel and dance music as jump-ups – the blues retained its bent-note or blue note quality, an inherent melancholy. But jump-up music became more rhythmic, evolving complex cross-patterns of polyrhythms, and more spontaneous in invention, spawning improvisation and syncopation around traditional chord changes and scales.

You wouldn't think it from the way that surfing is represented in contemporary culture – as a get-away-from-it-all form of relaxation, or a beach culture turning its back on the work ethic – but surfing is fundamentally melancholic. It is a 'kind of blue', a strange fascination that becomes an obsession. Not getting in the water makes you blue, but paradoxically, the whole tone of surfing sessions can be like a call and response with the sea that draws sailors' ghosts for company. When you are in your teens, surfing is all funk and strut, but as you get older and test yourself a little, those sea ghosts will try to run you down, and will haunt your nightmares. The top end of ecstasy in the perfect moment – the tube ride, long hang ten or big wave drop – is a small part of surfing's endless grind and challenge in paddling, duck diving, wipeouts, shark anxieties, bodily wear and tear (because the joints and ligaments give way long before the will), and the self-generated insults of extreme-challenge travel. Most surf trips have an underbelly. But I would have it no other way. This is not masochism, but living the blues, improvising life, making meaning.

Driving through Baja California's desert, a ribbed sandscape looms like a glassy swell under a torching sun. But these waves never break. They hover in a surreal sweat. Bleached by reflected light, my eyes trick me, until a searing wind snips the mirage into ribbons. Sand triple-coats the windscreen; tumbleweed races by. I blink, nostrils flare and smart in reflex. Relishing in the sudden lack of axle-grinding topes – Mexican speed bumps – I go faster down the empty stretch of highway entering David Lynch road-movie territory. I think of Lynch's adaptation of *Dune*, and imagine those enormous sandworms rearing up in front of the four by four. But, of course, there is just the hum of the surfboard straps and my worm eyes scanning the ever-receding horizon. I turn off-road on to a smooth sandstone track heading for the coast. I am scanning the surf, my eyes on the Pacific.

There is a blind bend. Another vehicle is coming the other way. I panic. A huge steel knuckle hits us with a shock punch. An eerie, all-embracing silence follows. A

Tijuana Moods – Baja, Mexico

feeling of hollowness – reduced to cold white ash. Both engines have died in the embrace. The impact bars have done their work. My conscience has been dented, but thankfully no one seems to be hurt. We check the boards, which are also unharmed. There is a mess of metal and both wagons are written off.

We are strung-out somewhere between Rosarito and Santo Domingo and some way from help. The day is getting hotter. After agreeing with the other driver (on a surf vacation with his Californian friends) that blame should be shared equally, we walk together, hoping to hitch a ride on the main highway, find a telephone and sort this mess. (This is before mobile phones became commonplace). The crew, and Californians, stay with the vehicles and strike up idle conversation.

As we stride out, the derelict wind blasts my face, and brings on a deep thirst; my throat is like sandpaper. Finally, we hear the clatter of a motor, and a dust cloud appears ahead, enveloping a heavily rusted Chevrolet pick-up. The wagon slows and stops, the driver indicates to jump in, and we ride without a word exchanged to the nearest gas station. The telephone is broken. So we catch an overcrowded bus, belching black smoke, and pass several abandoned and burned-out cars, some now skeletal, with their tyres gone and seats stripped out. At the next gas station I impotently, angrily, shake another broken telephone. But one of the pump jockeys has a satellite phone, and finally we are able to contact the hire company in San Diego. They agree to send a local insurance adjuster if we wait at the gas station. Reams of paperwork follow. A tow truck appears and we head back to the wreckage. The driver is straight out of a Sergio Leone film, with a mouth full of gold teeth. Auto-recovery is clearly the business to be in, because the curse of the baked Mexican highway and the light that plays tricks with your eyes will get you sooner or later.

It has been four hours since the crash. Not a single vehicle has passed by the scene, so our arrival signals the end of a period of mind-numbing boredom for the crew of friends after what was initially a good surf trip. The sun pancakes and quickly sinks below the horizon. The vehicles are inspected and untangled as we hitch up to the tow truck. The crew head for the breaker's yard, where they can sleep in mobile homes, while I ride to Guerrero Negro with the insurance adjustor. He says that our California-purchased, Mexican insurance does not cover all the damage. We will have to negotiate a van ride back to the USA for the following day to organize paperwork, clear up just what our liability is, and how the insurance company will pay the rest. We smell a scam, but there is little we can do but go with the flow. The adjuster points me in the direction of his cousins, who just happen to have a Ford van and are willing to drive all of us and our kit to the American border, a twelve-hour trip. They can set off in the morning and it will cost us $100 each. I sense a rip-off, but we are vulnerable gringos. After all, it is the Christmas holidays, and this seems to be the only option. They have us over a barrel. They will inevitably blow most of it on a big night out in Tijuana, hitting the rickety, corrugated-iron bars, necking José Cuervo, and then riding the haggard old donkeys, spray-painted for the tourists in black and white to look like deranged zebras. No doubt they will end up shuffling the night away with some señoritas on a sleazy dance floor to The Champs' 1958 surf guitar hit, Tequila.

Time is in abeyance on Christmas Eve morning. I wait at the motel from hell for the Mexican cousins. It is putrid. Not that long ago, we were surfing good Mexican waves, then camping out on the beach. We got fires going, stark against the mica-black skies, studded with cat's eyes. One night the brushwood was dying, so we proudly claimed a huge dead cactus and threw it on. It caught ablaze and we waited for the warmth to burst forth, but the cactus collapsed, whole, into a pathetic heap of white dust, which only served to dampen the remaining embers. We just could not get warm enough sleeping under the clear ceiling and thin skins. Now, in the unseasonal heat, I hanker after some of that chill. The rising sun is unremitting, and everything appears to wilt. Shadow offers little relief. I would swap with that cactus right now as I feel like a live ember that refuses to burn down.

The van arrives. An hour later we reach the scrap yard where the rest of the crew have slept with all the kit. I muse on the front gate, which has a large bull skull on it, horns intact. Maybe a matador wearing skin-tight pants, a silk jacket heavily embroidered in gold and a *bocorne* hat, fought him during one pulsating afternoon's corrida. Opening the iron gates, the strange whine is like the bull's last breath before the matador, agile like a surfer, cross-stepped towards him and sunk home a clean blade, the bull hypnotized by the man's confident poise.

A stiff wind peppers my face with stinging dust. Death metal is all around as hundreds of wrecked cars, vans, RVs, trucks and motorbikes rust away. I am grateful that we are in the auto graveyard and that our own bones have not been laid to rest in this red-earth backyard. The crew are covered head to toe in a sienna cloak, and when they remove their shades, they have stark, white rings around their eyes, as if ghosts lived behind those skins of dust. We load up. I pull shut the bull-skull gate, and step into the stifling van. We travel in silence for much of the next 12 hours. I zone out, dwelling on what has happened, my eyes fixed on the mesas and oily horizon in the distance. We only stop twice for gas. It is an intense ride, hitting blind bends at speed, and racing perilously close to the edge of the highway.

We finally arrive at the highway border. The cousins pull over, drop us and our gear by the side of the road, and collect their fee, their minds already on fast-forward to downtown Tijuana. We have to jaywalk over barriers with our load, but that does not seem to matter because we are still in Mexico, where the out-of-kilter is the norm, and we finally get in line to proceed through the border control on foot.

It is 11.30 p.m. on 24 December when I fill out my visa waiver forms, but 00.01 a.m. on the 25th when the passport officer checks my forms: 'Sir, step behind the green line,' he barks. Now we have left Mexico, the American surveillance mentality kicks in. Everything has to be in order. The *faux*-politeness grates. The date has totally baffled him. I try to explain that it was yesterday when I filled out the form, and now it is today, as it took some time to cross the line, but he does not like my attitude. He takes me into a room for interrogation. The confusion finally clears and we all stand beyond the green line – finally in California. We mock-toast Christmas Day. The Mamas and Papas' *California Dreaming* runs through my head, and the haunting flute solo by West coast jazz musician Bud Shank. This is a California nightmare (on such a winter's day).

We should be relieved to be back in California, but here on the border is one of the strangest places on earth, with desert behind us and a reclaimed desert ahead of us. Southern California is in many places 'a reclaimed desert' – from the lush golf courses to the concrete cities and shopping mall strips rising from sand, all watered by a vast irrigation system – and all built on a fault line. But Californians have turned geological instability and the fear of natural disaster into a lifestyle, as entertainment. Living on the fault line and the threat of the earthquake is transmuted into the excitement of the Disney ride and the Hollywood action disaster movie. Disaster is transformed into spectacle. And surfers have turned the wild Pacific into an area for recreation.

We have no money for a hire car, but the keys to a beach hut of a friend who is on holiday. We wake up on Boxing Day and use the bus service, and a lot of walking in between, to go surfing at Sunset Cliffs. My Californian dream has collapsed like that cactus on the fire in the desert. I have been all over the world, often to be greeted by great happiness among poverty and hardship in so-called 'developing' countries. But right here in the richest country on earth, travelling on the bus, I see the underbelly of poverty, of body and spirit. There are Mexicans living in squalor working the orange groves, paranoid about getting caught as illegal immigrants and therefore wide open to labour exploitation, and people from all backgrounds left behind, without health insurance, because everyone has a car in the land of stars.

I talk to a streetwise tramp in the seat next to me. This hobo has learned the art of survival by employing Californian values to challenge Californian values. Under his coat he is wearing an old tuxedo. He pulls out a mirror and combs his hair, explaining how he has perfected the art of locating private buffet occasions, turning up at the parties, blending in as an eccentric ex-businessman, and taking full advantage of the free food and drink. He would stuff himself, and then move on, to sleep anywhere for days with no meals. He gets off at the next stop, hides his coat and bag and starts walking, offering me a goodbye wave, on his way to a champagne lunch. The initial shock is tempered as I think of Jack Kerouac 'on the road' – a middle-class writer getting his material by jumping freight trains, hitching and sleeping rough. This is Kerouac in mock tuxedo.

We take the bus to its final stop overlooking the Pacific, walk along a sprawling feast of breaks, and gaze down on perfect 6-foot waves welling up in the kelp beds, spending their energy in long rights and lefts at Sunset Cliffs. This is the dark and light of California, a place that can make you feel dirty one minute and vital the next. By late afternoon, sets rise up against the spice-ball of the sun, and as I take off, I hang in shadow, and then kiss the red light as I hit the lip, remembering that bleached-out feeling of my first lone ride at San Onofre.

Despite the great waves, I returned to Cornwall broke and depressed, the Mexican crash replaying vividly in my mind. There are different kinds of deserts. I had left the desert in Mexico to hit another aridity head on in southern California, and now I felt arid – a desert of the imagination. I was gripped by melancholy, a permeating mood, a hollowness. The tip of Cornwall was packed in an envelope of drizzle, cloaked in a cold fog. And then the oddest thing started to happen – the more I tried to get back into a familiar routine, the greater the discomfort that ensued. The familiar seemed strange, refracted by the experience of travel, but not in an exciting or enticing way. Much as I loved Cornwall, it was as if travel had erased any notion that I had a home.

Out of the blue, I got a call from a friend in Canada. He told me that if I could get over to Fernie in the Rockies, he had a place to stay and a lift pass. He was setting up a ski and snowboard school. I could not resist the opportunity to cleanse myself in the mountains, and had not been snowboarding for some time. I had learned to snowboard in Canada during my gap year. But I did not have a penny to my name, and no surfing-sponsorship paycheques, or prize money chances for weeks. I filled my blue Volkswagen van with old surfboards, called up everyone I knew who might want a bargain, and drove around West Penwith selling them for paltry sums. When I had just enough to afford a train to London, an airfare to Calgary, and food for two weeks, I walked into a travel agent in Penzance and paid for the ticket in cash. Now armed with a mobile phone, I called my friend from the Greyhound bus to Fernie. We joined the first lifts with a fresh fall of snow. That thin, clean, high air offered a rescue remedy. I charged downhill, riding slopes like folding waves, and refocused on the present. My blue mood deserted me in this white-powder desert, and I couldn't wait to take that tone and lyricism back to the ocean.

Tone and lyricism is crucial in surfing and, of course, jazz. Miles Davis was a great bandleader – to complete the balance between the intensity of John Coltrane and his own, spare, open phrasing, he needed a player with uplift. The alto saxophonist Cannonball Adderley provided that sweet tone and lyricism. While seeped in the blues, Adderley also liked more of a positive rhythm and tone than many of the honking r 'n' b players of the time. Lester Young was the father of the lyrical end of bebop, straddling the swing and bebop eras of the 1930s and '40s. His tone was copied by a lot of white, West coast jazz musicians, such as Gerry Mulligan and Art Pepper. The player who took this route and made a signature mark was Stan Getz, who developed a unique, lyrical voice on the tenor sax without being saccharine. Getz could swing and managed to turn the otherwise mundane bossa nova sound into something that had body to it – lyrical, easy on the ear, and capturing the bobbing movement of swell in alternating high and low notes in phrasing, rather than running up or down a scale. The most beautiful stylists in surfing are lyricists. Never sweet, but phrasing with exquisite tone – moves that are just right but also have a strange, angular take.

Mexico's desert sound did not inspire me, even when I went back to compete at a contest in San José del Cabo at Baja's southern tip. It was not until a trip to Oman many years later, organized by John, and travelling with trusty friends Tristan, Zed and Emi, that I really 'saw' the desert, listened, and realized its beauty. This desert was neither bloodstained with oil-based conflict, nor the site of mass starvation. The Wahiba Sands were at peace, and the locals at peace with their fluid home, stretching beyond the reach of Middle East war zones.

Deserted highway – Oman

Oman's oil revenues have been cashed in to construct smooth tarmac – time's arrow is literally laid out as far as the eye can see. Skeins of sand hover like a glassy swell in a white-hot sea. Once again I face the mirage I saw all those years ago in Mexico, but I break through this wave as we gun from Muscat to the coast at Shana. The view drives me inward to ponder existence at the centre of a vast sky. It dwarfs any sense of self-importance. Here, the desert does not bring on a feeling of desolation, but of isolation. The desert is not 'abandoned' or 'discarded', as the dictionary definition suggests. Nor is it a place to be 'reclaimed' – the southern Californian perspective. To think of the desert as 'empty' is a conceit. For the local Bedu (the Bedouins of Oman), the desert is a rhythm, a sanctuary, a rich and intense presence with its intrinsic music.

'The desert is how you live it,' they say. 'The desert is freedom. It has no margins because our nomadic life erases borders. The desert is such that wherever you are within it, you are always at its centre and at your centre.' The Bedu see the desert as a fluid landscape, in which the future can easily be read. Like the ocean, the desert is a moving feast, and you must be able to spot its patterns and trends. No wonder we use the metaphor of a 'sea' of sand.

Zed Layson at prayer time – Masirah Island, Oman

In the warm, salty Arabian Sea, on the east coast of Masirah Island, real liquid 3-foot waves throw over a shallow right point. The burning sunlight magnifies dark spots that mottle the face. I recognize these rare rock outcrops as ophiolite. The sets look consistent, but a jagged bottom shape has contoured the waves in unpredictable ways. We paddle out for some closer fieldwork. Zed tests a wave and our initial fears are confirmed. Racing over the suspect rock, the section sucks up, pulls taut, and his fin breaks clean out with a striking sound – a keening note. He soon returns to the line-up with a new fin and an educated perception. After a flash of brilliance through an arcing turn on his burgundy-sprayed, egg-shaped board, he meets the same spot with more speed, but the bottom snags him again. This time he sacrifices some skin and has to pull needles of volcanic rock from nasty wounds in his feet and hands. The blues hound us but offer the ground for improvisation. Every wave shapes the imagination.

As the sun pours into the horizon at Hilf, the only town on the island, we check in at the Masirah Hotel. With a rival establishment soon to open, the owner has employed an energetic and quick-talking manager to set the standard. Following his flamboyant introduction, he swings an about-turn to show us around the hotel. With gangly limbs, high-waisted trousers and a comical walk, he is a mirror-image of John Cleese as Basil Fawlty of *Fawlty Towers*. Minutes later the act is complete when his socially awkward sidekick, 'Manuel', arrives. 'Manuel' darts around incompetently, trying to keep his superior happy, but is constantly bullied by him. All that is missing is the over-coiffed and acerbic wife, Sybil. But here in Islamic Oman, women remain a backdrop, a mystery.

'Manuel' is eager to impress in the hotel's restaurant, but his serving technique is hilariously clumsy. His poor command of English irritates his boss. A quick cuff around the ear is followed by a yelp and clatter of crockery in the kitchen. Under more pressure, he fumbles again while serving dessert. Our host apologizes – it is as if they had closely studied the *Fawlty Towers* scripts. But of course, John Cleese based these scripts on a real hotel in Torquay, and there is no reason not to believe that this is universal behaviour in similar establishments across the world.

A pastel-lemon sunrise throws a special light over Masirah's desert landscape. In places, the sand looks absurdly like snow. The sharp hills are flanked by the occasional stone wall that offers the eye some relief from the intensity of the sandscape. On close inspection, minute specks of blue azurite and green malachite dapple the rocks. The sea colour in the south-east is a direct match for these rare minerals. In the north-east it is filled with brown sediment from the gravel hills. A string of right points and rocky beaches are concentrated between Shanazi and Haql. But even at high tide, the waves spin over shallow and sharp rocks. Uneven sections catch me by surprise to raise their daggers. And on the outside, we catch the dagger of a small shark's fin raising itself above the water. We stare at each other nervously. As we finish the session, the fishermen come ashore with a frighteningly large catch of baby black-tips. Zebra and bullhead sharks also roam offshore, but we convince ourselves that the turtle population in the beds of sea grass will be of more interest to the predators than the bony bodies of surfers.

Midday passes, and a dry west wind picks up, beating back the normal onshores and raising temperatures to 40° Celsius and beyond. Even the resilient desert scrubs will retreat to their deep taproots, hoping the night brings dew. The camels come into their own – graceful in this setting, perfect evidence for natural selection. Omanis breed tall, long-legged camels famous for their speed and stamina. The Sultanate has a department for camel affairs, or, properly, camel racing. The best animals can get up to 30 m.p.h. In the flurry of dust at the start of a race, the less prized sometimes gallop off in the wrong direction, or simply stay put until someone pokes them with a lit cigarette. Camels are notoriously single-minded and choosy about whom they please. Their culinary tastes, however, are

Right: The camel trail – Oman

wide-ranging – they eat anything, although their favourite delicacy is sun-dried sardines. While I feed them bananas, they are just as interested in a parched piece of cardboard, which has fallen to the ground. As I kick it away, one of the camels shows her frustration. She stares down her nose at me, blinks through her double row of extra-long eyelashes (wonderfully adapted for keeping out sand), and flares a hairy nostril. Her lower lip stretches out six inches and shakes uncontrollably. She lets out a roaring groan, her cheeks puff out as she gathers saliva. I retreat, bent over double with laughter. The crew are in stitches. The powerful spit misses by inches, and is instantly absorbed by the hot sand.

Responding to a changing swell pattern, we board the ferry back to the mainland to head further north along the Al Wusta coast. We drive for hours, from Shana to Hijj, and then from Sinaw to Al Kamil, skirting the vast Wahiba Sands, stopping to walk a little and soak in the majestic landscape. The desert's barchan dunes seem to feather like waves as the wind whips across their crests. We try sand-boarding, but our boards simply sink rather than glide. Walking the desert is a powerful meditation – I attempt to walk like a Jain, with one eye on the ground searching for life, which must not be disturbed, and the other on the horizon. When you are so far out of your natural habitat, clues seem to be offered by the environment as to how to adapt. Here, to the naïve visitor, the message seems to be: listen and tread carefully, for the desert is alive.

The rogue American psychologist James Gibson described perception not as humans acting on the environment, shaping it perceptually according to their needs, but as the environment 'educating' our attention. The world works on us, or affords us perception, and we respond to its lessons. If we were to take on this idea, then we would not be so eager to shape the world to our desires, but, rather, to appreciate how the world educates us into her presence and beauty. This is so easily translated into surfing. Good surfers wait for the wave to educate their perceptions – to shape their responses. Others try to impose themselves on the wave, or perceive the wave as something they might shape – at which point they wipeout. Walking like a Jain must be like this – a heightened awareness at every step dictated not by your desires, but by how the world presents itself to you.

We make tracks for the sandstone right-hander at Al Ashkharah. Paddling out, my sight is saturated as the water reflects back a white sun. There is a slick wave with smooth rocks underneath. Outback, however, the lips quiver like that camel's, making top turns slow and heavy, instead of breaking hard to pump me down the line. But I soon recognize that this place must be read like the desert. You have to respond to the unique way in which the wave unfolds, and, once wired, this may be the best point in Oman. There is no good jazz without a keen sense of what others in the band are doing. The surfer is not a solo player but a soloist in a

Left: A permanent sand swell – Wahiba, Oman

Keeping cool – Tristan Jenkin, Oman, and radical equipment – Ar Ruways surfer

band that is the swell, tide, current, wind, and bottom shape. Surfing in a crowd or a group adds to this. A good surfer rapidly puts together these elements to work with them, honouring all the other band members and their contributions.

We spend the week educating our senses on excellent breaks between Ras al Hadd and Qurun, playing consciously bent or blue notes, but not bum notes or fluffed lines. At dawn, the offshore wind whistles through the desert wadis. In Ar Ruways we meet a lone ten-year-old Omani surfing a cut-down kite board. He lets us share a few of his waves. Hospitality is central to desert culture. Where sharing can be a means of survival, today's guest will be tomorrow's host. He does not mind us sneaking a few photographs, although it runs against the grain of Islamic law, which allows no representation of the human form. But he knows that for us the image is a keepsake, a memory not a religious transgression. From behind intricately patterned, half-closed doors, his friends laugh, and finally gather to form a crowd, cheering on the surfing.

Left top: Shelter from the desert storm – Tristan Jenkin, Al Ashkharah
Left bottom: Desert tip time – Al Ashkharah

After weeks in temperatures hot enough to boil blood, we drive back along the coast to Muscat. We move out of the sand dunes and into the hills, where flash rainstorms have cut wedges out of the landscape, like giant blades, that run to boulder-strewn riverbeds. We follow these, and soon we are back on those endless swathes of tarmac, through Qurayyat and climbing smoothly to Muscat. We pass some of Oman's ancient castles – mud-brick forts perched on desert crags – until the road breaks through the gravel-capped mountains that hem the capital. We stop to wash the dirt from the four by four after the thousands of miles we have put on the clock, and then follow the corniche leading to the port at Muttrah. The sun sets into a saffron sky. At the close of a great and instructive desert trip, there is the welcome cool of dusk. As night falls, the streets gather the smell of frankincense and sandalwood. The moon hangs noiseless like a silver sword, immaculate.

Left: Grand Mosque, Muttrah corniche, Muscat

12 Surfing Away from a Sinking Ship

Herman Melville said that no true place is ever on the map. I take this to mean that the soul of a place cannot be contained by the political boundary of a country. Like many post-colonial nations, Mauritania is scarred and searching for an identity by trying to link tradition with progress. These giant forces, pulling in opposite directions, give places a twist, a hump, a sense of discomfort. Mauritania is anchored on the North West African coast like a docked ship awaiting repairs, one side gathering industrial rust and sinking into the deeply cold Atlantic, the other – sand-swamped. Travelling brings you face-to-face with contradictions, like local fishermen who never learn to swim (maybe deliberately, so that they drown quicker if shipwrecked). In Mauritania, such contradictions form a lifestyle. While cherishing its nomadic roots, such tradition is broken on the steaming wheel of the iron-ore trade. While respecting that the very land itself shifts with time as mountainous dunes are reshaped by ceaseless wind, people attempt to lay down political boundaries, these markers no longer moving with the wind, but with the decisions of bureaucrats who no longer live in the heart of the desert but in run-down cities at the rim. And there simply is no map for the location of landmines that litter the access routes to a wealth of incredible waves on Mauritania's Ras Nouadhibou peninsula in the north.

I was listening to one of Art Blakey's Jazz Messengers' blazing versions of *A Night in Tunisia*, and thinking about alternatives to Morocco's popular and now crazy hub. I gazed at the atlas opened to North Africa and contemplated the Mediterranean coastlines of Libya, Egypt and Algeria. But the unknown quantity was Atlantic Mauritania, and John invariably goes for the unknown quantity.

The hot band on this gig was John, Emi, Tristan and French friend Erwan Simon from Brittany. There would be a good chance of excellent surf in the northern reaches, but it was hard to ascertain if this war-torn area was politically safe. There were territorial and border disputes with Morocco, and civil strife in the country itself, the southernmost extension of the Western Sahara. Mauritania's border with Morocco is a territory of old colonial Spain, abandoned in typical post-colonial style, and then claimed equally by Morocco, Mauritania and the Polisario Front – an Algeria-backed Sahrawi nationalist organization fighting for control of the land. Battling for what appears to be one of the most sparsely populated areas in the world may seem strange to the outsider, but this is home-

Clipped wing cranes – Nouakchott, Mauritania

land to its champions, albeit a disputed place littered with landmines and generating a shape-shifting border created out of the mind-maps of ministers.

It may be just a trifle, but when I learned that 'Nouadhibou' rhymes with 'Malibu,' the lure of Mauritania kicked in. I had a mental image of empty, reeling waves spending their force at the apron of fishing villages, but this dissolved when, in the midst of our research, came a news headline from Al Jazeera: 'Four French tourists shot dead in Mauritania'. They had pulled off the road to enjoy a picnic, inland from the capital Nouakchott, but refused to hand over their money to bandits who suddenly appeared to spoil the party. Days before our departure, another Al Jazeera alert turned our anticipation into collective anxiety: 'Three Mauritanian soldiers shot dead by armed men in a clash in the north'; then: 'Dakar Rally cancelled due to Al-Qaeda threats'. But our crew had to balance this with the outlook gained by seasoned travellers – always respect local traditions, comply with the military, and keep as low a profile as possible. Mauritania is not the comfort zone that Morocco has become. This is precisely what brings us here – edgy travel at the land's edges and brilliant corners.

Our close, on-site mapping of Mauritania's edges begins with the beachbreaks of Nouakchott (pronounced 'Nwak-Shot') – 'the place of winds' in Hassaniya Arabic.

A sharp north-easterly slashes at the wave faces, and the water is colder than we expect. Duck-dives beneath inky sets bring us sharply to our senses. We all feel the chill. A long-derelict industrial wharf shelters the take-off. It turns shallow and hollow as the tide pulls away from the pale sand. Along the pier, fishermen cast long nets into the line-up, pushing us deeper behind the sections. The swell runs through the shoal, and we follow the contours of the waves as they frame the catch. By afternoon, the wind has coaxed the cold shadow at the back of the sun into a front-stage appearance, and we freeze at the thin edge of the desert, putting on our fringe theatre – a dress rehearsal for the days ahead.

Nouakchott's recent coastal sprawl has been poorly planned, built on land slowly subsiding into the Atlantic, so that upwelling salt water has already claimed new neighbourhoods, abandoned except for a few feral cats. The rest of the city creeps inland. Hastily constructed to become the capital, it has low-walled, canvas-roofed houses, the signature of the nomad, uneasy with settled life. We dodge the 'traffic' – braying donkeys chased by stick-wielding charioteers. As the load of scrap metal from boats and cars becomes burdensome, the drivers crack the whip harder. Battered Renault 12s are held together with rope. The bone-dry air slows rusting, and skeletal cars inherit the look of the afterlife in this life, their skins peeled back.

Dust and sand bank up against bare, bleached walls of rudimentary buildings bristling with hi-tech satellite dishes. Among the ranks of silver-inlaid boxes on display in the *foire artisanale* (craft market), men sell mobile-phone holders and telephone cards – welcoming us to the global village. Swaddled head to toe in robes, the locals greet us with warm smiles and vigorous, clasping handshakes. Right now this feels like one of the safest capital cities I have been in. The sharp cracks induced by snapping crab claws at dinner time seem like the closest we will get to the sound of gunshot. There is a confluence of orderly, Arab North Africa and the south's colourful Black Africa, where stiff geometric patterns meet bright, swirling robes. This sharp contrast and complicated conversation also shows between those who appear to float rather than walk, and those who appear to shuffle, their slippers wearing thin, perhaps reflecting those twin forces of progress and tradition. Imagine somebody shouting a whisper and you will get the picture. Or Listen to Lee Morgan's *The Sidewinder* – a strange, angular phrasing like a snake moving across sand that resolves itself at the end of each phrase in a generous pause.

The sky is still jet black as we load the two four by fours with local surfers and drivers, Thierry, Nicolas and Brahim, to head north to Nouadhibou. Along the way, we encounter police checkpoints, so familiar in post-colonial Africa. The policemen sit idly in tent entrances, drinking mint tea and smoking. Thierry stops the car, leans his head out the window, and shouts, '*Salut Chef*,' a common French-Africa greeting. He morphs into rapid-fire Arabic, explaining that he runs

Brahim at the wheel – Mauritania

the business that makes all the police and army clothes in Mauritania. This has an instant impact, and we are waved through with broad grins. At the next stop we hand over a bundle of multiple photocopies of our passport details, and again we are waved through. These military mantras have replaced the traditional forms of greeting among nomads. After a cluster of checkpoints, we hit a five-hour stretch of straight asphalt breeching empty desert, and make good time. I think of how strange this 'route 1' mentality must be to people used to the elliptical voyage, moving out in an arc from the oasis, and curving back by a different way.

The desert is a restless body, unable to sleep because of the nagging wind, and we ruffle the body even more with our racing tyres, so unlike the soft-shuffle, slow moving caravan. Thierry talks about the time he spent with the nomads, living with camels, travelling away from a water source and back in huge petal shapes across the sands. The nomads see the minute differences in the dunes. They know a place by subtle changes in grain size and textures, an educated pattern recognition. They can always find their way, even though the landscape shifts dramatically over time. But with borders drawn across paper maps in bureaucrats' offices, most of the people have been deprived of their nomadic existence. They now live in Nouakchott and Nouadhibou under the alien spell of 'development' and 'settlement'.

Police checkpoints appear with unnerving regularity as we enter the sprawling cement and sand of Nouadhibou – industrial, gritty and lined by a ship graveyard. Iron ore and fishing are the arteries and veins of Mauritania's fragile economy, and here in Nouadhibou is the grinding reality of proto-industrialism and its inevitable waste. We bypass the city for the west coast before sunset. Trying to breathe in a sense of place, we get instead the stink of rotting fish. We stop to speak to local Imraguen fishermen (who are nomadic, following schools of red mullet) about the border and the landmines. The border no longer runs north to south down the narrow peninsula. It has shifted to a new west to east direction, although this is yet to be recognized by the UN. We stick diligently to the tracks, steering over the railway line that brings iron ore from Zouerate to the port, then through the neglected and dangerous minefields. The terrain becomes extreme. In the Toyota Hilux, Brahim powers through the sand and sharp rocks as if born to it, with an eye for the sinuous track, just like surfing.

Flocks of black-winged seagulls wheel, in great clamouring rings. As we finally see the coastline, our jaws drop. Sandstone pointbreaks and slabs stack up in both directions. The choice is overwhelming. Chilled deeply by the Canaries current, the water is even colder than in the south. Our wetsuits are too thin, and we shiver between sets. As the sun drops, we hurry back across the peninsula, needing the light to keep to the tracks, in order to avoid the landmines. The after-glow of surfing good waves is cruelly squashed by the vile stench of Nouadhibou, the town ringed by dry-roasted garbage and plastic bags.

A cold night sets in, and the wake-up is an impressive set of duelling muezzins calling the faithful to prayer. We drive to the southern tip of the 40-mile-long peninsula. At Cap Blanc, a spectacular shipwreck clings to the sand, the most impressive of hundreds allowed to beach in blatant insurance scams (repeated in other parts of Africa). The north-east wind howls, but we revel in the multitude of pointbreak set-ups, until we are confronted by an armed soldier, who tells us that it is illegal to pass through La Agüera without a permit. This once-beautiful colonial Spanish town, overlooking a bay and natural harbour, is now bullet-holed, burned-out, abandoned, and blown over with sand, another legacy of 'border mentality'. Among the ruins is a well-manned Mauritanian army post where no-one shall pass without the requisite papers. For silver-tongued Thierry, on this occasion, the fact that he makes the General's uniform does not offer enough credibility.

Fortunately, Thierry knows a government official in Nouadhibou. After a successful meeting he arranges our permits with the General. We are able to explore new surf territory – our own small coup. La Agüera was built when colonial Spain established an air base here. Modern maps still use a border between Mauritania

Left: Whispering dunes – Nouadhibou

How high can you go? Erwan Simon – Ras Nouadhibou peninsula

and Spanish possessions that runs down the middle of the Nouadhibou peninsula, but that now appears to have shifted to the north. So why are the Mauritanian troops in La Agüera? The town formed part of an area administered by Mauritania before it gave up claims to Western Sahara. It is an anomaly, a place left behind, outside the Moroccan wall, abandoned by both Moroccan and Polisario forces. It has become a political symbol for Mauritania, which does not recognize Morocco's claim to the Western Sahara, so it is guarded by a Mauritanian military outpost, although not formally Mauritanian territory. Welcome to Melville's 'true place' that is never on the map. The simulacrum is pervasive – map and territory no longer align.

Armed with permits, we arrive at La Agüera, a strange black hole where time stands still and snipers linger at the window holes, fighting a territorial war that appears to benefit nobody. Soldiers appear from the shabby barracks. The General insists on escorting us as we explore the area. He tells us that there is a high

Left top: Two directions at once – Tristan Jenkin, La Agüera
Left bottom: Steaming into the wreck – Ras Nouadhibou peninsula

concentration of landmines around the town, but the tracks are well used and we do not stray from them. At first, he seems hostile, but changes his tone dramatically as he watches us surf one of the excellent right pointbreaks. There are long waits between sets that follow a desert rhythm, sinuous slow-time. But the waves are consistently good when they arrive. The General attempts a coup on John's camera work, but is shrugged off by John who hates that kind of interruption to the expert rhythm of his art. The General reappears with his own video camera. From the slabs of sandstone he starts to dictate the session, demanding that we all catch the wave together, then shouting to 'go further' when I kick out. And he practically orders me to stay in when I am surfed out, wind-stung and hungry. I split a baguette and fill it with tinned tuna. Flies inevitably gather. I am not sure which is more frustrating – dealing with the flies buzzing about my sandwich, or the General buzzing at my ears, asking countless questions. I can see he is itching to have a go. He asks if he needs to be able to swim to use the boards. We surf more sessions under the General's dictatorship but, unable to swim, he does not tackle a ride. Unlike the flies that continue to bug us, his intensity lessens; he is genuinely friendly, and thrilled by surfing. We get to like his angular ways.

The contradiction of Pacific surfers attempting to meet martial ways does not go unnoticed. I think of the long-standing paradoxical alignment of the military with surfing, such as the great Californian breaks (like the hotly contested Trestles) right next to military camps. Recall the B-side of the Surfaris' *Wipeout* – 'Surfer Joe', where: 'Surfer Joe joined Uncle Sam's Marines today/ they stationed him at Pendleton, not far away/ they cut off his big, blonde locks I'm told/ and when he went on manoeuvres, Joe caught cold'! Not the most complex of lyrics, but a nice reminder of how the military have appropriated access to some prime surf locations. The run-ins between the military and surfers attempting to gain access to these locations is a central part of the folklore of surfing, signalling the struggle between two cultures.

By early afternoon, Nouadhibou is buzzing, the stalls adorned with hanging camel steaks, and spilling over with fruit, vegetables, spices and pungent dried fish. But all is not well. A woman appears from a shop, swathed in blood-red cloth. We stop. She looks angry. She walks closer, inspecting us. 'Américain?' she asks. 'Les Etats-Unis,' answers John. A long pause ensues. 'Américain, BLAHHH!' she says, sticking out her tongue and giving an aggressive thumbs-down. In response to each of our nationalities, she says, 'Italien, BLAHHH! Français, BLAHHH! Anglais, BLAHHH!' A small anti-Western protest gathers around her, and we slowly slip away. At a distance, we burst into laughter, but this is a nervous response. From her perspective, the decadent West deserves scorn after the string of stereotypes that constitute 'orientalism'.

Roused by ululating calls to prayer, we eagerly head for the coast and its promise. The north-east wind pierces through every layer of clothing. It stirs up the

Mint tea for two times three – Nouadhibou

desert to create a thick haze. Our eyes clog with sand, but Brahim's knowledge of the dunes restores our sight. He connects us with the surroundings, a fluent reader of the landscape's script. He engages us with a permanent smile, and communicates with impeccable timing through his regular mint tea ceremonies. Every glass is perfectly poured. Every significant marker in the desert is pointed out with detailed attention and respect. He leads us to a majestic collection of dunes, the largest haloed by what looks like a mist spraying from the crest. Walking up to the summit offers a stark contrast to human folly and territorial dispute. It is so overwhelming that we collectively withhold comment. Hiking down the face, deep and loud phantom groans appear to rise from beyond the dunes. We think it is the iron-ore train echoing in the distance. But as we descend further, the groans increase. We realize that the sound is from the dune itself. The whole mass creaking and heaving is at root fractal – just single grain rubbing against single grain, multiplied up, until an entire dune sings out and drones. Driving away, we do encounter the ghost train now fully materialized as 100 carriages, broken by engines, dragging tons of iron ore, offering an ugly contrast to the eerie but wondrous groan of the dunes.

Wreck 'n' roll – Ras Nouadhibou peninsula, Mauritania

Our journey arcs back to another graveyard of ships. Right-handers reel off hulls. We are drawn to the shallow reef with a sharp, hollow lip smacking against the northern ship, snipping its metal atom by atom. But I cannot resist the novelty factor of the peak that wedges against the southern vessel – visualizing surfing from a sinking ship, Malibu style. I take off right by the wrecked boat, and a soul arch mimics the angle of rest of the wrecked vessel; then we all paddle to the faster wave on the other side of the ship. The faces are burning blue, like run-around gas on Brahim's burner that brings his mint tea to the boil. The larger, smoking sets spin out respectable tubes, the large ones swing wide and bite into the ship's stern. The mid-sized waves expire in deep water right next to another hull. Tubes pinch tight, then punch us out, just before the boat blocks trim and forces a tight kick-out. Erwan darts from the lip and launches an aerial as if on a methane geyser ignited by the friction from his flying board. He falls close to the landing, hits the reef but pops up intact, with a badge of honour – boat-wreck rust daubed on his wetsuit.

Eventually, I tire of the loud clatter of sets striking the steel boats that shower and pancake to silence, and paddle in from this strangest of breaks among the ship graveyard, a post-industrial surf break. Our trip to Mauritania ends with this paradox – surfing wrecks. Industry laid to rest. Surfing wrecks lives – it grips you, it is addictive, and you follow, wide-eyed to a coastline littered with landmines but rich in pointbreaks, your home life always on a knife-edge as the compulsive urge to travel grips. It is not your mind that gets pulled by the magnetic field of those edges to the world, those ledges that drop into deep-water ocean, or those gentle aprons that soak up the spill of beachbreaks. Rather, it all begins with itchy feet, where the need to scratch is transferred on to the land, to reveal what is beneath the surface of that terrain that is new to your senses and over which your footprint looms large as 'global traveller'. This is not the footprint of Friday, that causes Crusoe to panic and, in paranoia, to defend what he now sees as his own island. Rather, the footprint is from the native of the island, and the traveller's footprint is the offender.

History moves to two broad kinds of music simultaneously, and life gets caught up, for one reason or another, in a particular rhythm. The one I have always avoided is the regular beat, the long march, the structure of authority that recognizes only the regular form of military music: one-two-three-four, right on the count. I prefer moving around the beat in the inventive forms of jazz, play-ing just behind the pulse, or anticipating the beat, creating openings and space – relaxed intensity. Syncopation. There is complexity in the space created as you lift off the beat, like surfing just off the high line, just behind the hook. This is not going to war, but learning to dance. Surfer Joe refusing the military, growing his hair, finding ways to surf the 'off-limits to surfers' break, using nonviolent guerrilla tactics. This is part of the larger pacifist movement of 'Multitude', giving voice to those marginalized by global capitalist exploitation, inspired particularly by brave eco-warriors.

We soon return to the north of Mauritania, to the 'official' Western Sahara – a huge parcel of shape-shifting desert sand, reforming itself in the post-colonial vacuum, and also carrying the terrible legacy of conflict, filled with landmines and a powerful military presence. The 'real' Western Sahara is not a country, but a self-governing 'non-territory', run by the Moroccan military, with a certain autonomy granted to the indigenous Sahrawi people. This place typifies our global paradox: we live in an age with so much potential for positive cultural exchange, yet war and strife are everywhere. And not just real wars – the language, images and metaphors of war and violence permeate each and every move. It is an irony that even medicine, the healing profession, uses war metaphors so readily – 'war' on illness, 'fighting' disease. And surfing, outwardly a sport embracing tolerance and participation, thrives on 'rip', 'tear' and 'shred' metaphors, adding to aggressive localism and tribalism.

Along a dry backbone of coast, sets rise like black-bodied whales, show sharp white spines, and split open in dazzling runs down an empty point, raising music

Not an air out of place – Breton Erwan Simon, Western Sahara

that enjoys the length of the keyboard. Tristan, Emi and Erwan are now experts at playing improvised runs against the grinding motion of the sea. They are jazz surfers, improvisers, out of the loop of localism and unnecessary rip-and-tear mentality. Watching, I turn to shore, and in the distance I notice a skinny man in a pale blue cap walking goat-footed down the high cliffs to make his way down to the tide-line – that indelible smile fringing a sweeping bay. An inflated tractor tyre inner-tube hangs over his bony shoulder, and he wears a torn wetsuit, the legs too short. On the beach he slips his feet into a pair of well-worn plimsolls neatly sewn into plastic swim fins. The inner-tube has a wooden base, and serves as a makeshift boat. He climbs in, holding a blade and twine. After another long ride to shore, and a shorter walk over the tangle of mussel-covered rocks, I am now pad-dling out for another wave, heading for the channel, and he is soon kicking beside me in practised style. With his spine turned to the swell, he works his way through a section of foamheads, using the rip current to get out back. He disappears for about an hour, checking crab pots, then settles at the sweetest peak and picks a wave. I think he is going to wipeout, but he kicks, arches his body and surfs right to the sand, his 'boat' alive with a catch of giant crabs.

We paddle in to meet this skinny salt on his home sands. A mop of curly black and silver hair tops his tall frame. His name is Drousi, and his smile reveals a mouthful of chaotic, yellowed teeth. I know that he knows things about the sea that even a seasoned surfer will never grasp. Drousi clearly loves the sea, not as something to be conquered, but as a greater presence to be respected. We accept his offer of boiled crabmeat, and as we crack the claws, a cartoon-like, perfect six-wave set runs the length of the bay, each wave cracking as it folds over, without a soul to share its muscle, a virtuoso drummer practising alone.

The village and shoreline are linked by a colony of bright blue boats, a huddle of tents and a display of sun-bleached rugs. We surf this point for days. Drousi tends his crab pots. Our Sahrawi driver makes mint tea over white-hot charcoal smouldering in the sand. Some of the local Sahrawi singers reel off folk stories from memory, with great composure. They know the tune perfectly, and so can improvise around it, to tell the story in a new way. Sahrawis respect the desert as alive, but sparse, and so tread carefully, finding a place of poise. Out back, the concentration of the set stretches out the whole length of the wrapping point. Your board does not have to rip, tear and lacerate these gifts of the sea, but can cymbal-ride like the drummer tapping a ringing beat, and then splashing the cymbal – not a crashing sound but a spread of colour caused by a rising or dipping sun. Another hand makes patterns on the snare drum; the skitter of the board that is controlled freedom – slides and stalls, nudges and hints, and then a sudden crackle as a deep turn is popped into the routine, called for by the way the wave itself dictates the ride. Not a gouge, but a seabird turning and dipping; not forcing the moment, but living the present. I do not see myself as going to war. Why fight the wave when you are inevitably a loser? Why not dance with it, and follow its unfolding gifts?

With a changing swell pattern, we say goodbye to Drousi and his brilliant corner of coastline. We give him a new wetsuit and head towards an enticing peninsula. The midday sun cooks the highway and melts the mind. Soldiers diligently clear swathes of landmines by the roadside. Suddenly the pincer movement of conflict that has gripped so much of Africa in the wake of colonialism nips at our heels. At military checkpoints, the Moroccan soldiers speak in arrogantly caustic tones to our local Sahrawi driver. War feeds war. Against a backdrop of diplomatic stalemate, as the UN strives for a solution to the dispute between Morocco and the Polisario Front, Morocco has encouraged tens of thousands of small-scale fishermen settlers from the north, and spent heavily on port infrastructure, to consolidate its hold on the contested land. This is likely to destroy a few surfing breaks with harbour construction. At the same time, many Sahrawi villages in the south have been burned out, and the people moved off in elaborate and detailed long-term Moroccan visions to develop and govern the area for tourism.

But can tourism thrive in a post-colonial region gripped by a military mentality, where authority figures always get their way? There is a cold logic to war. As a state of exception, during times of war even democracies revert to authority structures. Those who want to maintain a permanent state of authority and hierarchy like to see war or conflict as the norm, rather than the exception. It gives them an excuse to indulge their marching-music mentality.

A narrow ridge of asphalt runs alongside a flat, gently arcing bay, and we taste the mouth-watering spray of three waves spreading across hundreds of metres. The road ends at a Sahrawi fishing village, where white boats are launched and landed, as the heavily regulated octopus fishing season gets underway. We take the Land Rover back along hard-packed sand, but our driver explains that despite the easy access this is military land and we will soon be kicked out. Another cluster of waves gather, skirt the rocks at the head of a low-slung point, and spin off right so mechanically that they resemble a Rick Griffin comic strip. But even the seabirds do not gather by the take-off spot. There is a taboo at work. It is tangled with war. I think again of Trestles and San Onofre in California where the military have denied access. I remember once surfing at San Onofre when a huge explosion went off at Camp Pendleton: 'That's the sound of freedom for ya!' commented one local.

The insignificant-looking military base ahead suddenly spits out a group of soldiers who clearly mean business. They order us to leave immediately: 'No authorization.' Surely, we say, this suggests that we can get 'authorization' as we did in La Agüera? Determined to achieve a similar small coup, we endure numerous meetings with the tourist board, developers and government officials, hoping to get right to the top – to the *Commandante*. We eventually arrive at the regional government palace, scheduled to have an audience with the Minister. The imposing architecture dwarfs us – the eye drawn towards a scarlet ceiling. Stained glass windows and mosaic pillars repeat and radiate, rhythmically. The patterns are intricate and detailed. The grandiose courtyard fountain and crystal chandelier suddenly tips me. We are all out of our depth, just travelling surfers, low on the hierarchy. Our confidence drains, and we collectively fumble the occasion and miss the opportunity. I feel the sand between my toes, the salt staining my eyelashes, and know my sinuses will drain tellingly if I stoop. Our surfer outfits surely fail us in this ostentatious setting, and despite our best efforts to play the 'promoting tourism' card, we are denied authorization to gain access to arguably the best (although most fickle) wave in the Western Sahara. The alleged, and ludicrous, excuse is that the presence of 'radar' at the military base makes authorization to surf there impossible. Suddenly, we know the meaning of getting 'under the radar'.

Right: Notes on the stave, and two sets of blue – Western Sahara

We realize that we are trying too hard, moving too high up the ladder of bureaucracy to gain access, and decide to go for a grassroots approach – bribery of the troops. We buy cigarettes, chocolates and dates. We park up by the entrance before the straight stretch of road that leads to the Sahrawi village and beach access. The whitewater from a set smokes in the distance – tantalizing, the call of the siren. The soldiers welcome the smokes and snacks, but when the issue of authorization to surf the wave is raised, they say we have to visit military headquarters. We do, and again arrange a promising meeting, possibly with the *Commandante*, but an officer explains that we need to go to the regional government. We have come full circle, and confirmed our theory that when the military is the norm rather than the exception, all works by hierarchy, but nothing really works at all, as it is frozen in that hierarchy. It is a self-serving process.

Examining the swell forecast, with only a few days left, it is clear that the very last afternoon of the trip will be prime to surf the military base. We need to displace the war mentality with dance, with jazz, with art, or at least with artifice. We put together a formal-looking letter with the names of all the officials we have met, explaining what we are doing. It will not be a fake letter of authorization, but a written documentation of our attempt to seek authorization. Regardless of what it says, we figure just the gesture of a formal piece of paper might play bureaucratic pinball and buy us enough time to ride a few sets. We plan to go surfing first, and then face the consequences, waving this improvised piece of paper.

We settle close to the fishing village, the boats overflowing with a fresh catch of octopus, heading for the freezing factories and then export to Japan. We suit up, like black notes ready to walk all over the score of the uniformly green sea, and paddle out. John starts shooting, the improvised document at the ready. Passing fishermen wave at us, to warn about the danger of the military base. But my senses are elsewhere, inspired by the different melodies of each wave; the way the lines smack the sea's surface as the lip folds over, like a drummer smacking rim-shots as the horn player ups the tempo. I drop down into the pocket for a long, drawn-out ride, now playing right on the beat, but swinging rather than marching. Dance moves meet arcs, not angles, in swooping roundhouse cut-backs and full-bottom turns. The vocabulary is fully exercised on this long, curving and luscious wave. It is a transparent pro-peace protest.

After a quartet of solid sets, one of the army officers walks over to John. Armed with our piece of paper, John casually hands over the document, as if we have every right to be here. The officer walks away, back towards the military base. We keep surfing, hearts pounding. John keeps 'shooting', and between waves and strokes I see the paper being handed over to someone in the head office overlooking the take-off zone, who will likely call the *Commandante* and maybe then there will be another, more sinister shooting. Two more sets steam in, a third, a fourth and a fifth set, Tristan goes, Emi goes, Erwan goes, and we revel in the unexpected pleasure. This is the 'perfect wave' for me because of the context – a hard to be, indeed an impossible to be brilliant corner. We are winning the war without striking a blow. We are following Sun Tzu's advice in *The Art of War* to focus on strategy, not combat. This way, we invite the unexpected, the unusual, the improbable, engaging with the essence of an out-of-the-way place and its inhabitants. This is surfing with a complex touch of law-breaking and law-making thrown in.

The base suddenly erupts. Men appear from the office, whistle and wave, now extremely agitated by our presence. The fishermen motoring back home continue to express their concern. We pack in a few more rides. The top military cat appears from the office and begins walking down along the beach towards John, exuding authority. We know that our game will be up at any minute. Thankfully, he appears to speak calmly to John, who coolly packs away his lens and begins walking away along the beach towards the village and our wagon. The other army officers start waving and whistling frantically at us all to paddle in. We disobey only because there is a lull, a gap, a drawn-out, painful flatness. The officers continue to push for our attention. This is a naïve gesture, because we simply have to wait for a wave to go in. They wave back. We begin to wonder what will happen if we get arrested. Finally, a cluster of waves arrives and we ride them all the way down the sand bar for hundreds of metres, knitting and knotting turns.

Just out of sight from the military base, I paddle across to snag the very last edge section. A wall rears up. I walk the nose, hang five, hang ten, stand bolt upright, raise my right hand to my forehead and perform an old-school 'El Saluto,' until I hit the sand: a tongue-in-cheek salute to the paradoxes of life on this little orbiting globe, filled with war and waves and the badge of the beret, worn tight by military types, worn jauntily and loose by jazzlife hipsters and beats.

13 West African Highlife...
Let Freedom Ring

Ringing guitars over rich horn riffs and upbeat tunes – highlife is Ghana's surf-dance music, infectious and uplifting. It embodies the characteristic optimism of Ghanaians. Hi-Life International's famous album *Travel and See* encapsulates Ghana's soul. 'Music to wake the dead,' say the reviews. 'Travel and see' – what great advice. And this is just what I do, along with John, Randy and Emi. We find a coast that awakens the senses across the whole spectrum, and then challenges sensibility. Ghana is beauty and the beast – a rich, vibrant culture with great natural resources, and rolling right pointbreaks, but a creeping, insidious pollution problem.

Ferrous oxide. Red rust. Rivers of the stuff seep from shipwrecks just offshore. Perfect little peelers run off the hulls, reel in and mix up a little more red rust to dissolve in the already muddy waters. 'These hulks were here, rusting away the last time I was in Ghana,' Randy recalls in disbelief. 'And here they are, still festering.' I think of Neil Young's *Rust Never Sleeps*, and turn it over in my mind as 'rust always seeps'. I turn to Randy and nearly call him Rusty. I am already infected with the stuff. 'Fancy a wave, one of those little peelers?' 'No chance!' we all say – the water is way too polluted, hanging as a dark red mirror under an intense blue sky, cancelling health and failing to pull the brightness into itself. Nobody wants to look into that mirror close-up. No surfing away from a sinking ship here.

I shake that morose Neil Young out of my head, and tune in to the local upbeat hubbub. Fresh in the 1950s, highlife was influenced by European jazz dance bands and pop, then sent back to Europe as a raunchier, guitar- and horn-inflected lyrical sound through a second-generation wave of Ghanaian emigrants in the 1970s. Highlife was one of several idiosyncratic African takes on pop and beat music that included Zairean Soukous, Nigerian Juju and South African Township, exported and popularized as a first wave of 'world music'. Close family friend, pioneering art and music filmmaker and writer, Mark Kidel, who filmed and promoted the first wave of Malinese 'crossover' musicians, conceived the original world music festival with Peter Gabriel, culminating in the acclaimed WOMAD (World of Music, Arts and Dance) movement. The fathers of highlife – London-based Hi-Life International, and Ghana's own African Brothers and Mohammed Malcolm Ben, recorded classic tracks in the early 1980s that play on themes of the ever-present paradoxes of African politics. How does a country gain an identity after

Joining the band – Fete, Ghana

years of imperialism, years under the thumb of the white race? Freud said that the repressed returns in a distorted form – as neurosis, psychological insecurity.

The rust ride was a poisoned apple none of us wanted to taste. Now we are hungry for waves. Labadi Beach is the obvious bet, the epicentre of tourism in Ghana. The greeting is refreshing: 'Is that a surfboard? Wow. *Akwaba* (Welcome).' Surfing's obscurity here is bizarre, considering that Bruce Brown filmed a touching sequence in *The Endless Summer* at Labadi. Californians Mike Hynson and Robert August gave lessons to crowds of local Ghanaian kids. In the grip of the Cold War, 1960s world leaders could have learned a lot from this social icebreaker. No politics or false diplomacy, just the universal language of laughter and shared skill. Surfing so often transcends politics in a search for a simple, often healing, cultural exchange. The whole fishing tribe was so enthralled that they chanted, 'Hang ten! Hang ten! Hang ten!' as if it would be the ultimate objective in their lives, or at least a mantra guaranteeing good times.

Apart from the odd visitor, the formative surf film failed to inspire surfers to travel to Ghana. The magazines are certainly a commanding influence upon surfers' travel choices, and most head for the more powerful breaks of South Africa.

European surfers, and those on around-the-world tickets, will also check out Morocco. It is not just the lure of the waves in these other parts of Africa, but the centres of gravity already created there. Morocco was once an exotic and interesting surf destination, but now, like Goa or Kuta Beach, it is also a place to hang. For all their supposed nonconformity, many surfers are, like most tourists, eager to make for the hive and join the throng. We make the most of our first stomp in Ghana, paddling into grey-green surf. But this is not the roiling pointbreak we are searching for, it is just the supporting band, so we head on after a stilted session, although we are pleased to get wet.

The following morning, driving east of Labadi, heavy clouds gather overhead. Below the buzzing-hot guitars and the harmonies of the horns in highlife, is a slow, rooted bass, thick and heavy, like the rolling tide of pollution that wants to engulf African nations. Soon, the bass will dominate, and that bright ringing tune will be dulled, unless the inevitable westernizing and industrializing of Africa does not deal with its dark side. Industry of any kind is inevitably bought at a cost – just 'travel and see'. Beyond Ghana's busiest port, Tema, the coast takes on a strange aura. Only the outline of wreckage is visible. One after the other, grey phantoms stagger into the distance, a ghost fleet. Under constant strain from the Atlantic, metal fatigue grips huge freighters, sliding into the drink. And here they will gradually dissolve. Instead of being broken up at a wrecker's yard, the ships simply come to rest and ungraciously fall apart at the seams. Once again, decent waves break from the hulls and between the dagger-like sterns and jagged metal. This must be one of the world's most bizarre, tantalizing, but unrideable, surf breaks. You would have to be drunk or stupid to paddle out. We pass everything from a nearly intact vessel to a mere keel peeking above the water. Some are splintered open from what look like titanic explosions, leaving the hulls awkwardly twisted, frameworks exposed like the ribcages of a rotting carcass. Others are prised apart, as if Neptune himself had used his trident to open giant soup cans. They look like marine parodies of Richard Serra's landlocked sculptures. The sea runs red where the sinking hulls slough off their oxidized layers. Rust never sleeps, rust always seeps.

Fish-smoke from ovens in Tema rises above the serried vessels. I ask the fishermen how the ships came to their pitiful ends, but they just nod their heads and look blank, as if there is no expression that can encompass this spectacle. The locals no longer pay them attention as they have been a fixture for so long. Over the years, inventive salvage has given the ships a second life, reincarnated as nails or cooking pans, a slightly ludicrous but resourceful reduction of the juggernauts to everyday commodities. A steady offshore wind carries with it the chatter of women at work, and a horn honks from a battered car, sounding eerily like a contest hooter, calling us to go surf. But despite the peeling waves, the sea just looks too unwelcoming, too abused, too much like a dumping ground. The mood

Hidden fruits – Tema, Ghana

changes as we pass through the heart of Accra where a corner, packed with giant wooden carved bananas, grapes and pineapples, displays a sign 'Coffins made to order'. I begin to appreciate the Ghanaians' sense of humour – fun is paramount here, even in death. Not 'Life is a bitch – you work, grow old and then you die,' but 'Laughter and friendship see you through the sad times, and then you die as a fruit!'

Accra is a sensual city, a place developed for the body rather than the mind, an outdoor life. There are vendors and buyers, those who cook and those who eat, and these roles may be quickly reversed. We walk, loiter, drink Star beers (another good label for Randy's collection), and a local encourages Emi and me to try the *fufu*. Thankfully, unlike some African cities, Accra has a reliable electricity supply, so we can see what we are eating. On this occasion, the clarity is unfortunate. It is a bowl of greasy tomato and onion broth with chunks of 'mystery meat' – cows' intestine, goats' lips, maybe dog. I pick out a doughy, pounded cassava ball. It is lubricated with oil and slithers down my throat. I retch. The local tells us that *fufu* is so ubiquitous in Ghana, their version of the nursery rhyme 'Polly Put the Kettle On' is 'Effua put the fufu on... It's time to eat... Ekow took it off again... We all ran away.' I can taste why.

First to the line – Fete, Ghana

At dawn, I change some money, and switching each dollar for 10,000 cedis instantly swells one's confidence. We go west through Accra and see a paradoxical show of wealth – swish cars, swank cell phones and palatial mansions complete with security guards and ten-foot-high walls. This is one of the most progressive places in Africa. The ostentatious presidential palace puts all the other explicit signs of affluence to shame. And this simply intensifies the shanty-town squalor on its doorstep, which spills over the eroding cliff side almost into the Atlantic. Goats with swollen bellies wander the alleys, desperate for scraps; chickens with patchy feathers barely raise a cluck; flies crowding around open sores plague skeletal dogs. Yet amid the paucity and pollution is an abundance of happiness. Pride and poverty walk hand in hand – open sewage gathers right by the beauty salon called Hallelujah Hairstyles, next to Heavens Above Hair Cuts. Women walk out radiant with shea butter. As things seem to fall apart, so people keep up appearances.

Ghana is a country that brings you to your senses. Music to 'wake the dead' is a good metaphor. My smile turns to a sigh as I focus on the crumbling, old colonial fort now operating as a prison. It is a terrible reminder of the slave trade.

Ghana had the highest concentration of slave posts anywhere in the world. The prison is so overcrowded that inmates hang out the windows, battling for space. Local boys play a football match in open freedom on the dirt park nearby. I join in. Their clothes are scant compared with mine, but they have a wealth of spirit. The goalkeeper dives, but misses the save. Goal! He collects the ball; he has slashed his knee and the cut is the colour of the sea below – iron in the blood. The sinking ship sloughs off more layers, and the sea runs red: rust always seeps; rust never sleeps.

We continue west to Senya Bereku, a slave fort converted into a hotel with a breathtaking view over an enticing, long, rolling right pointbreak. Ghana is packed with points good enough to attract any surfing crowd. But you have to escape Accra to find cleaner seas. The old slave castle looks peaceful, covered with a coat of white paint and draped with palms – a picture-perfect façade for a place that was an accomplice to one of the greatest evils of humankind. The forts began in the sixteenth century as small trading posts in gold, ivory and spices. Access to the interior from here was easy compared with swampy neighbouring coastlines, and building materials were abundant. But a human darkness, a rusting heart, was born here. Forts became slave prisons, shipping Africans to the Americas. Next came the long road to freedom with the liberation songs of Harriet Tubman, Frederick Douglas, Rosa Parks, Martin Luther King, Malcolm X, Jackie Robinson and Muhammad Ali. Fittingly, Martin Luther King visited Ghana on the occasion of its independence from Britain. Against this dark background, you appreciate even more the bright ring of highlife, its wonderful celebration of melody and rhythm, moving away from the blues so often associated with the history of slavery. Highlife is a formal refusal of chains, not a lament.

At Fete point, we find a lavish peeler that is faster, longer and better than Senya. The readily accessible Ghanaian point surf finally brings the trip some high class. The pushing tide starts to create clean walls and zippy sections. I can hear a distant mix of sounds from the village. The sea is the real composer, and I follow her rhythms – classical on-the-nose poses take on quirky angles as I shadow the dances in the local bars and simulate their moves, yelling and hollering sweet sighs as the sound of freedom from slavery taken to the ocean's skin and tattooed as blue notes in sharps and flats. During the lulls, I watch fishing boats sailing past. This seems idyllic, but, as I ride in with the tide, again I encounter the mix of sublimity and poverty. Clean moves are no longer the order of the day at the beach that also serves as the village toilet. As the sets swamp the rocks, the odour is intense, and we quickly seek some distance.

Back at Labadi, nightlife does not creep up on us, but bursts forth with vigour. We toast Ghana, calling it the Jamaica of Africa. Walking through the crowds on the sand, Rastafarians pound bongos, their dreadlocks wheeling through the air like snakes. The drumbeat is contagious and bodies begin to gyrate, hips wiggle and feet stomp. Break-dancing begins. Windmills-on-the-floor, head spins. This is not highlife, but hiplife. The youth of Ghana have developed their own form of hip-hop, fusing highlife and rap. Give Ghanaians a topic and they will turn it into music that will ripple through your body and back, as cross-rhythms. If they can translate their music into surfing talent, which will surely happen, they will bring a new grace to agile wave-riding, a quality sadly missing in many zap-and-snap-era wave dominators. And the native surf community might be encouraged to combat their pollution problem as part of that music-making, to give the sea some vital tone. Paddling out for my last surf in Ghana, the highlife rings around my head and runs to my feet, turning to cross-steps to the nose. I try not to break the backs of waves, or hack at the opal faces, but dance with them. On my last ride, I tuck under the lip as if entering one of those fruit-shaped coffins with a smile, and then laugh out loud, dancing away from danger. I am high on life in Ghana. Travel and see.

Other parts of West Africa have not enjoyed the recent freedoms of Ghana. The great jazz drummer, first bebop pioneer and then master of all styles, Max Roach, an African American, studied the rich drumming cultures of Africa first hand, and summed up his learning in the phrase 'Let freedom ring!' (which the alto saxophonist Jackie McLean used as the title for one of his best Blue Note albums). The sticks of skilled, loose drummers, as extensions of the hands, run around the kit, on fire. They form patterns, rings and polyrhythms, with tom-tom rolls accented and punctuated by snare-drum snaps. In music, there is nothing closer to surfing than drumming. But what if your drumheads are cruelly torn, your snares snapped in two, your cymbals bent, your bass pedal crushed – worse, your hands severed in torture? Africa has also been war-torn. After the colonial period and its terrible history of slavery and greed, when European countries withdrew from their African colonies, there was often not peaceful transition. In some areas, old rivalries were renewed, and in others, new conflicts set ablaze. Often, the music stopped, the beat froze, and hollowness emerged. Highlife was one side of the fence. On the other, life was desperate – entirely about survival. Child soldiers were recruited and trained to fight in wars they did not understand, their parents already dead from the conflict. Many grew up knowing only terror, rape and hardship.

It is a short flight from Accra to Monrovia, the capital of Liberia, burned out from a bitter civil war. And that rumbling drumroll and a pocket of anticipation develops deep in my gut again. It tightens and knots, as if I am about to paddle into a wave too steep, too hollow and too ugly to deal with. I had drunk bad water en route to Ghana's airport – stupidly mixed up my bottle with the taxi driver's tap water. I feel a sweat coming on. Robertsfield Airport focuses my energy, and I stave off the sickness for the moment. Below me is a sea of blue helmets – UN peacekeeping soldiers. The city has just turned on its streetlights for the first time in 15 years. President Ellen Johnson-Sirleaf announces that this symbolizes the country's journey from darkness to illumination.

Emerging from the airport, an ominous atmosphere develops – a human weather system, where collective tension gathers as a storm cloud about to burst. Kids who, for years, have been toting guns or fleeing from their homes in fear of their lives, have grown up knowing only civil war, and now have to adjust to a civil life. The psychological hurt is etched deep in the country's psyche, creating an understandable atmosphere of paranoia. We are the only tourists here. We need the collective cool heads of experienced travel to defuse the situation. Hardly a mob, but something sinister seems to be happening as the men, huddled in a tight group, weigh us up. We model the diplomatic way, deliberately sitting out of the way – 'ghost whites'. Keep a low profile, stay cool, weather the storm. The descending cloud, mirroring Liberia's tensions, gets thick, dark and nearly splits open. Flustered and sweating, UN employee Dominic arrives. He is our contact in Liberia, and we have been organizing the trip with him through telephone calls for months. We escape for Monrovia without interrogation or violation.

There is barbed wire everywhere. My throat and stomach sympathize as the body's prickly defence rises against whatever I picked up from that bad water. The road is also sick, pocked with bullet holes; there are burned-out homes, and alongside it is littered with rusting vehicles. The past chaos rebounds ahead, as a lorry spins out of control and crashes – the inevitable fate of poor maintenance. It is tragic that, in the wake of the senseless slaughter, more deaths will occur in the rebuilding of a nation, because, after the martial madness, nothing in the civil world works any more. Billboards offer stark reminders of the horror of war: 'Raped – A woman is your friend. Don't beat her, cherish her.' Another: 'Stop mob violence.' And another: 'Use the law.' Apart from the UN peacekeepers, I cannot see evidence of the law. This is a wild frontier in recuperation.

A positive sign of recovery is evident as we pass a group of women dressed in strikingly colourful fabrics, elegantly navigating open sewers. Character shows in perfect postures. If you could bottle the beauty or grace of movement, this would be your line.

The pressure inside my stomach becomes unbearable. I cannot hold back the bug any longer, and the moment we arrive at Dominic's overcrowded family home in New Kru, I burst in the makeshift bathroom. I spend the night tiptoeing back and forth to this rudimentary, no-flush facility. Waves of cramp work through me and I feel like the lingering spirits of war casualties are tearing my senses, replaying their histories for the privileged visitor. This depth of empathy I can do without. But I survive the white-ghost ride, and walk out to a morning landscape haunted by the neighbourhood's dead, the living still mourning their loss. This is a place where mobs of child-soldiers, high on palm wine and *dagga* (the local dope), killed without mercy. Villages burned for over a decade. There is a lingering smell, like rain on ash. A heart of darkness beat here for longer than people care to remember, and the shadow is only just passing. A new heart is

Local stand-out – Alfred Lomax, Robertsport

being massaged to recover the pulse of ordinary human interaction, free from suspicion, fear and terror.

Sheet rain stitches itself into the road, further cracking the ruined concrete. Between downbursts, we load up the Toyota Land Cruiser. The engine smokes and the day is already sweltering. Finally, we drive away from the mess of concrete into tangles of dense trees, and then towards a fringe of luminous yellow sand. Every coastline has a spot where the nervous system gathers and shows through – a place that pulses and demands that you engage with its raw beauty. Robertsport offers its treasures. The ruined Cassava Beach Hotel sits awkwardly on the beachfront as evidence of the destruction caused by war, its windows long since shattered, and then the eye is pulled to the Atlantic, as sets of waves unravel for hundreds of metres. With some local kids up and riding it is easy for a surfer to read these waves as a symbol of hope for Liberia. There are five remarkable left pointbreaks. Here is a place that can and will benefit from sensitive surf tourism, to aid a country rising from the ashes. This does not feel like we are penetrating deeper into a heart of darkness, but rather, seeing a country breathing more easily, her rainforest and surf cleansing the air.

Point of many returns – Robertsport, Liberia

It is dusk, and we will have to wait until dawn to taste those peelers. Africa is a good place to challenge the instant gratification mentality familiar to the psyches of the so-called 'developed' countries. Erecting tents in front of the 200-year-old silk-cotton tree, and hearing the cracks of the waves rifling at third point, it is obvious that Liberia's quality makes it West Africa's promised land for the adventurous surfer. The rain clatters with increasing urgency, preventing sleep and daring us to go outside to meet its force. Then a vicious downpour, seemingly targeted right at us, causes the tent to collapse. The sky gods are emptying their vessels, or hanging out their laundry, and must be laughing at our mortal vulnerability. Emi and I battle the elements to harness the tent ropes to the resilient silk-cotton tree branches. I wear my skeleton on the outside, Haitian-style, getting scrubbed. Our tent flaps like a flag on a Tibetan spirit pole.

In the early morning, a blanket of dark cloud spreads across the sky, seeming to seep into the near-black, silk-surfaced waves. We paddle out. The current is relentless and it is difficult to duck-dive under these hard-driving corkscrews. A bigger face rears from the horizon and the wave gallops, showing its teeth. Before I get to my feet, the lip bites, picks me off and pitches me into seething

West African Highlife... Let Freedom Ring 183

foam for a punishing hold-down. I am relieved to pop up to a lull, and paddle back out with purpose, thinking carefully about where to sit for the next set. This is a demanding break. I focus, feel the drum beat, and regain confidence.

Beat is the cumulative series of punctuations, the stresses, the accents – how you hit the lip and rebound, what you do at the full extent of a roundhouse cutback, the point of recovery at the end of the floater that keeps momentum in the ride. Some accents are soft and subtle like brushwork on snares, but usually they are played hard and deep like rolls on the tom-toms, or sharp, as wake up calls, like rim shots on the snare drum. There are no better masters of beat than Max Roach, Roy Haynes and Art Blakey – the snap, crackle and pop of drumming. From Roach and Blakey you will learn everything you need to know about accents on the deeper toned tom-toms and bass drum. From Haynes you will learn about the crisp cross beats on the snare drum. The beat is not just the drummer keeping time, hammering along. This is for squares. The beat for jazz is an accented beat, a beat that leads and draws patterns.

We explore the five pointbreaks and their patterns with the local kids, who learned to surf on boards left behind by UN workers. I recover from my stomach bug, sleep, eat, and my surfing makes music again. Maybe the spirits are appeased, having seen us survive the night's torrent only to engage with the ocean's torrents by choice. The gods love madness, courage and style, perhaps in that order. I dart through arcing turns until my thighs burn and shoulders cramp. Fatigued, we huddle around the evening fire and make friends with the Grebo fishermen, who act as security, and cook for us during our stay. Surfing makes the kids tingle with enthusiasm. I am blown away by how well they all take to the water. I have never seen this much interaction with waves by other youngsters in Africa. The Gross brothers (all seven of them) are gripped by surfing. Momo stands out – thunderstruck the moment he tries my board. I watch his first lone ride. A sticky set picks him up and glues his board. He springs to his feet and follows the motion of the wave as it unzips down the line. He gains speed and crouches lower. His stance is instinctive – if you could bottle natural style, this would be your best-seller. It reminds me of my first lone wave at San Onofre; gripped for life. Momo's learning curve is exceptional throughout the short time we are privileged guests at his family's beach. He pounces on me to borrow my board every time I come out of the sea. He is a natural, it gets under his skin and only another ride can satisfy the itch.

After surfing unbelievably long, grinding lefthanders all day, we grill mackerel on an open fire with the locals. Momo begs me to take him home to Cornwall for

Left top: Thor's Day – The day after Big Wednesday (the following Thursday) – Gross brothers, Robertsport
Left bottom: Walking the line – with Emi Cataldi, Robertsport

Washing in the creek – with Momo Gross, Robertsport

just one week of schooling. I tell him that he can learn a lot right here. This place needs him to look after it, to help with recovery. Momo is beginning to appreciate the value of Robertsport's natural resources, understandably tainted after a savage period of war. Education that is sensitive to tribal tradition is key to the future. The locals thank us for sharing surfing with their sons. We brought friendship to a nation recovering from trauma.

I reluctantly pack up, my back knotted like the silk-cotton tree roots that I slept over. The dawn oozes out of the long wound where the sky is sewn to the sea. We take off from Liberia. The lights have been left on. I see those perfect waves zippering around Lake Piso, and throwing deep foamheads into Robertsport. Certainly the local and visiting surf community will have grown dramatically by the time I return, as I plan to do. Those priceless waves will offer a wonderful, renewable resource, in the development of eco-sensitive surf tourism. Dominic and others have since started to achieve that. Rising from the ruins, surfing looks like a beautiful, singular alternative to war.

I arrived home from Liberia deeply affected by what I had seen, and more, what I heard about the suffering, loss and human destruction brought about by the fighting. Child soldiers have grown up never knowing a peaceful existence, where hatred was more prominent than love, and now they are trying to make sense of a 'normal' life, rebuilding a culture. I thought about the Gross family just about scraping a basic living from fishing, and a rush of mixed-up feelings ran through me that I could not resolve. For weeks I dwelt upon stories I had been told, such as Robertsport continually changing hands among different warring factions, each one torturing, raping, then forcing children to join the warlords. The local kids had lost friends in the conflict. Drunk on fermented sugar cane, they were given machine guns and ordered to fight without mercy. Some escaped to Monrovia, walking at night along the coast for weeks to avoid being kidnapped. This scenario would be replicated in other parts of Africa, particularly the Sudan. Some of the Robertsport kids then had to spend six months hiding in Monrovia to avoid the same fate under a different warlord. Here they heard about cannibalism – gunmen eating a victim's heart in the search for courage; and children wearing wedding dresses into combat because they thought it made them invincible. When they finally returned home to Robertsport, and the war ended, surfing became their sanctuary, their escape. This is the purest example I have come across of how surfing can offer healing and hope.

Nothing is certain in an unstable post-war climate, but among the uncertainty, these Robertsport locals have found identities – as surfers. Liberia's resources are potentially lucrative – iron ore, gold, diamonds, rubber, and abundant rainforest. But these are non-renewable, and relying on them seems to invite corruption and the tightening of the post-colonial grip, as another African country becomes an outpost of the 'developed' world, continuing the saga of the rubber-industry outrages perpetrated by King Leopold's Belgium – Joseph Conrad's 'heart of darkness'. Given this legacy, it is no wonder that much of post-colonial Africa fell into local turmoil as countries attempted to regain a sense of identity. Mixed into this is the bigger global conflict between religions, which is also at the core of a great deal of identity confusion. I saw where the human darkness of slavery was born, and where its rusting heart resides, shipping Africans to the Americas, before the long road to freedom and the most important breakthrough of human spirit. I praise the liberation songs that collectively call for the upholding of human dignity in the face of oppression.

West Africa was a wonderful precursor to the most intense and exciting trip that I have yet taken, to Haiti, the travel story that opens this book. If anywhere represents a displaced people's struggle to challenge the legacy of slavery, it is Haiti. After a slave rebellion and war of liberation against the French colonialists, Haiti was born in 1804. Haiti forced me to test limits, take risks, mentally and physically. These risks seem frivolous, however, in comparison with the resilient human spirit of every Haitian I met. I had to raise my spirit to a new awareness to

Spirits of the future – Haiti

meet Haiti's presence. The trip felt like a culmination of everything I had learned and seen through ten years of extreme travel, all focused into one experience of being turned inside out. Only in Haiti could I have answered the most improbable of surf travel conundrums. Without hesitation, I confronted the impossibility of transporting all our kit on the small internal aeroplane flight from Port-au-Prince to Cap-Haïtien. I talked my way on to the runway and persuaded the pilots and airline manager to load our baggage of long- and shortboards on to a nineteen-seater twin-prop Turbolet. The hold was minute, so the only option was removing four seats from one side of the aisle. Surfing, travel and jazz had taught me all about improvisation, perseverance and unwavering focus on the present, because, with the right attitude, anything is possible. Seats unbolted, passengers clambered in, boards filled up the space and we made it to Cap and had the ride of our lives.

Above all, the spirit of Haiti made the impossible possible, because this is a place where people deliberately live at maximum complexity on the edge of chaos. Haitians ritualize life to maintain this intensity. With too much intensity, it all falls into chaos; with too little, the moment does not achieve its potential. It is like surfing – riding something of maximum complexity the right side of chaos, the blue-water wave, as it falls and breaks into whitewater; trying to remain in balance on one side of the wave's curtain as the lip flings over, knowing that if you make one erratic move, you will be picked off and combed across a razor reef. Engaging with a dynamic system at its most intense naturally offers high-energy risk and danger together. Charles Mingus' *Haitian Fight Song* begins with a crisp, clear theme, then slowly develops into a more complex but dynamically structured composition, and finally wails and stings. Likewise, the waves in Haiti also wailed and stung, so complex engagement was essential to survive each ride. They whined and we dined. And then, just as easily, the roles were reversed, as they dined on us in stinging wipeouts, and we whined. This is the essence of work-song. Mingus describes how the deep feeling in his composition could only have been born out of identification with the oppression and suffering that has led all those who have come out of slavery to make the most out of life. For Haitians, the 'other side' that is chaos is the constant presence of death. There is a semi-perme-able membrane between life and death that is readily crossed. I swayed on the edge in Haiti, saw that the spirits inhabit busy places, hung on the cusp, brushed danger, and looked into a beautiful darkness – a trip at maximum intensity, but not in chaos. Another Haitian proverb I heard was 'Kay koule twompe soley men li pa twombe lapli' – 'The leaky house can fool the sun, but it cannot fool the rain.'

Back home, I could not ignore the impact Haiti had on me. The weather of places, their atmospheres, their pressures, will seep into your leaky psyche and inhabit your being. I felt like I was wearing my skeleton on the outside and that my nervous system was stretched over that. I was infected by stored trauma from a certain kind of raw exposure to that country and its soul. I felt that country's history impress me with a force that left me reeling. I could only deal with that by going surfing, perhaps escaping, but also returning to the practice field to play jazz and to explore more newly visited brilliant corners.

John Coltrane and Sonny Rollins – perhaps the two greatest tenor saxophon-ists in modern jazz – gained lasting respect for their live performances, where big, long, awesome solo codas of 20 minutes or more were not uncommon. Both the stamina and powers of invention needed to maintain that level of intensity of improvisation are remarkable, and only came with diligent practice and passion-ate engagement with the music. But they also came with a deep sense of history. Coltrane described immersion in such solos as spiritual: he often felt possessed by a holy ghost, so that the music came through him, rather than claiming that he was the source. Coltrane's massive, sweeping sound is the tone of spirituals, the blue-black body of the history of slavery. Claiming surfing as a form of jazz, an improvisational art, is also a move to re-vision surfing's relationship to slavery and oppression, and to invite a black holy ghost back in to the sport as a spirit of invention and a sound of freedom.

14 Kick-out Coda

If 'thinking jazz' offers a way of surfing, perhaps the *avant-garde* of surfing rests with travellers who surf the unexpected, sometimes on unexpected equipment, in unexpected ways. If the *avant-garde* is experimentation, then perhaps radical travel is its jazz voice in contemporary surfing, playing not just off, away from, and around the beat, but entirely off the beaten track. My jazz has been the song of travel and discovery.

Along the way the ocean has knocked me senseless, torn ligaments, ruined my sinuses, reduced my spectrum of hearing, dragged me across infectious live coral reefs, held me down so I am close to drowning, and engineered a face-to-face encounter with a tiger shark. But such bruises generate a kind of wisdom, and they are suffered because the rewards of surfing are immense. Surfing has opened me up, split my skin, widened my horizons, and closed me down, because any obsession restricts your involvement in other aspects of life. The sea has focused my restless, complex personality and given me calm. Travel has permanently reddened my eyes, but layered experience upon experience in building character. Surfing has been my life practice – all other activities, including my academic and writing passions, have been built around it.

Every surfer will have a story about the tensions that an addiction to surfing can bring to a partner, particularly one who does not surf. I have suffered these tensions, and brought frustration and anger into past relationships through my dedication to travel. At the same time, travelling has taught me that there is nothing more special in surfing than being a local, having a family, and that one should cherish home breaks, home life. I have never tired of the vaulting granite cliffs at Gwenver in West Penwith, the bright skirt of sand, the changing seasons, and the familiar faces that keep me sane, acting as an anchor. I have grown to love the winter squalls; the pungent coconut, pineapple and vanilla haloes of gorse in early summer; the first cuckoo, the dipping swifts catching insects on the wing, the hovering bird of prey momentarily stitched to the sky. The central gift of travel has not been to shape me as a nomad, but to make sweeter the return home. And when new guests arrive at my home, I have vowed to offer them the same hospitality and friendship that I have experienced from locals in tucked-away brilliant corners of the world.

When I least expected it, I met Sandy, renting a house perched on Escalls Cliffs between Sennen and Gwenver. She gave off a fresh energy and vitality and a beautiful zest. She was a keen surfer, widely travelled, worldly-wise, and her family name, uncannily, was 'Cornwall'. She radiated enthusiasm, and could take the pulse of any situation, but she also had the perseverance to grind through the bad times. We spent an unforgettable time living on the cliffs, looking out on the wide sky and approaching weather fronts, the changing beach shapes, the pattern of swells, wheeling gulls and bobbing cormorants. At night we would light the log fire and memorize the phosphene collision where moonlight met wave spray. We would watch the ribbon of whitewater build around the castellated cliffs, and with the rising tide, surf together where the vaulting cliff met its fate, wringing out sound from the sea's body, until the beach was just a tight, high line.

Sandy and I travelled through Europe, Africa and the Caribbean. Between waves, we danced in bars, found the animal pulse of newly visited coastlines, and surfed for our sanity. We took the wave as a message for life – you simply have to accept that when the curtain falls, and you are deep inside, you may or may not make the exit. But we also sensed that some deeper ground was being formed that would offer continuity, longevity, and clarity. Neither of us wanted the logjam of the city, and we vowed never to serve Mammon, selling our souls to the daily grind. Despite the passion for travel, we were locked into West Cornwall, where the land had gripped us and we had learned its code, calling it 'home'. Our common love was the ocean, and we saw ourselves as sea life.

We were married outdoors, at my parents' house – Poldown, at Escalls Cliff – on a summer's day with a cobalt-blue sky and a strong easterly wind combing the sea. We bought a cottage close by, further along the cliffs at Gwenver. Here, I watched our daughter, Lola, being born. At four months, she lay on the nose of my longboard in Barbados and we paddled into hot, six-inch peelers. She smiled, I hooted, Sandy cheered, and we repeated it in summertime at home. Maybe one day she will stand on her first green face, alone in trim – a ride for life. Maybe she will crack the code of hanging ten. But above all, I want her generation to succeed where ours is still failing – to establish ecological habits for a lifetime.

The more I travel and surf, the more I see surfing not as escapism, but as a grounded and positive way to flag up our pressing global environmental concerns. The globe is steaming, people are starving, ocean pollution fingers further along the world's coastline, and the ugliness of the bottom dollar meets you in the most unlikely of places. Surely all of us can inhabit the space between responsibility and aspiration and ideals. I do not want Lola to grow up carrying the burden of a previous generation's irresponsible attitudes to the environment. I want her to have the choice of surfing in clean, unpolluted water, and of sharing that choice with those who live by, and with, the oceans across the world. I hope she grows up to respect and care for all life, leaving footprints that others would wish to follow. And I hope that this book will inspire people to think jazz, to improvise, to be imaginative, unconventional, and to make radical bright blue ringing notes. Let freedom ring.

Siargao Island, the Philippines

First published in 2010 by
Alison Hodge, 2 Clarence Place, Penzance, Cornwall TR18 2QA, UK
www.alison-hodge.co.uk   info@alison-hodge.co.uk

ISBN-13 9780906720806

British Library Cataloguing-in-Publication Data
A catalogue record for this book is available from the British Library.

Cover design: Christopher Laughton

Book design and origination by BDP –
Book Development & Production, Penzance, Cornwall

Printed in China on paper produced with elemental chlorine-free pulp, harvested from managed sustainable forests.